# Typographic
# Milestones

## Allan Haley

BOLD
York

Library of Congress Catalog Card Number 91-47005
ISBN 0-442-23642-5

Printed in the United States of America.

Designed by Monika Keano

Van Nostrand Reinhold
115 Fifth Avenue
New York, New York 10003

Chapman and Hall
2–6 Boundary Row
London, SE1 8HN, England

Thomas Nelson Australia
102 Dodds Street
South Melbourne 3205
Victoria, Australia

Nelson Canada
1120 Birchmount Road
Scarborough, Ontario MIK 5G4, Canada

16 15 14 13 12 11 10 9 8 7 6 5 4 3 2 1

**Library of Congress Cataloging-in-Publication Data**
Haley, Allan.
Typographic milestones/Allan Haley.
p.   cm.
Includes index.
ISBN 0-442-23642-5
1. Type and type-founding—History.   2. Type designers—
Biography.   3. Printers—Biography.   4. Printing—
History.   I. Title.
Z250.A2H18   1992                           91-47005
686.2′2′09—dc20                             CIP

---

*Illustration Credits*

Claude P. Garamond, p. 25. New York Public Library
Picture Collection.

John Baskerville, p. 39. Courtesy The Bettman Archive.

William Addison Dwiggins, p. 85. Reprinted permissions
for the AIGA Dwiggins Exhibition Keepsake, 1957. Photo:
Robert Yarnell Ritchie.

Eric Gill, p. 91. Reprinted with permission from *The Letter Forms
and Type Designs of Eric Gill* by Robert Harling. London:
Hurtwood Press, 1976.

# Contents

# PREFACE

Those who molded and formed our typographic heritage were dynamic, frequently outspoken, and at times, relatively eccentric. At certain times they faced seemingly insurmountable obstacles on the paths to their goals. They rarely, however, took "no" for an answer. These were men and women of passion and drive. They were relentless in their quest for excellence, and many times this inability to compromise affected their personal lives—sometimes negatively.

*Jan Tschichold* appeared to be a scholarly, gentle man. To look at him, you might have thought that he was a kindly professor of Latin, or perhaps classical literature. Certainly this was not someone given to harsh words or radical thought. Tschichold was, as he appeared, soft-spoken, genial, and cultured. He was also branded by his peers as a radical, renegade, and self-contradictory agitator.

*John Baskerville* was cranky, vain, and scorned convention. He has been called a dilettante and an eccentric. Fellow printers disapproved of him, his type, and his printing. Baskerville broke the rules of his craft to create what he believed was perfect printing and, in doing so, alienated almost all of his contemporaries.

*Beatrice Warde's* business card read "Director of Publicity, British Monotype Corporation." This doesn't, however, begin to describe the breadth and value of her responsibilities and influence within Monotype, or her contributions to the typographic community. While she never rose above a middle management position, Beatrice Warde's influence on typography and typographers was, in many cases, more pronounced and far-reaching than that of the corporate officers of her employer.

Baskerville, Tschichold, Warde, and the others who helped to create the heritage of our craft were vibrant, ambitious pioneers of their eras.

I learned about these people a little at a time and over time became intrigued with the parallels in their personalities and ambitions. I also became aware of the similarities between the adversities they faced and the challenges facing the typographic community today.

I first wrote about these pioneers of typography in a series of articles called *Typographic Milestones* for the quarterly journal "U&lc." The purpose of the articles was to provide a link between the typographic past and present and to provide some insight into the vitality, dedication, charm, and even fragility, of those who helped to build our typographic heritage. This book is a compilation of those articles. It is, however, just a sampling. There are many more passionate advocates illuminating the history of typography. My hope is that the light of their passion is maintained by current practitioners of our art and craft.

# ACKNOWLEDGMENTS

I am deeply indebted to many people without whose support and help this book would not have been possible. First there is my family, who understood my need to write and tolerated the time it took from them. Second there is Aaron Burns, who taught me, first hand, what being a passionate advocate really meant. Last there is Karen Nagle, who typed my manuscript with patience and skill. Acknowledgment is also due to Sid Timm, Carol Danielson, and Vincent Janoski who edited my work and made it better —much better.

# I
# EARLY GIANTS

# Johann Gutenberg

## 1394–1468

A young man from a good family of comfortable means got himself into trouble and had to leave his hometown. He moved to a nearby city, where he managed to get along, on the surface living respectably, but preoccupied by a scheme to make his fortune. To finance this plan, he began to persuade people to lend him money. The scheme was somewhat complicated and required the services of several accomplices, whom the young man found among the itinerant workers and students who populated the city. He swore them to absolute secrecy; no one beyond his small, select band was to know of his plan or its development.

But the enterprise did not progress well. The young man needed increasingly more money—which he borrowed. Several of his accomplices left to pursue their own versions of the scheme. And finally, a catastrophic event forced him to flee the city and return home, deeply in debt and haunted by the idea that would eventually destroy every normal aspect of his life.

Thus begins the story of Johann Gutenberg, a man surrounded by controversy in his lifetime and shrouded in confusion after his death. What was he working on before he returned to his hometown of Mainz, Germany? Some say that it was a simple plan to sell trinkets to religious pilgrims. Others claim that it was something much more important. How was Gutenberg able to continually persuade people to lend him money? Why did he eventually go bankrupt, never to enjoy the fruits of his labor? Did he really do all the things for which people give him credit?

## WHO WAS JOHANN GUTENBERG?

Ask any first-year graphic arts student to identify Johann Gutenberg, and you will quickly be informed that he is the Father of Printing. Yet Gutenberg did not invent the craft. Neither did he invent the printing press, nor printing ink, nor even movable type. Gutenberg's Bible was not the first printing done with metal type, nor was it his most important contribution to the art of communication.

There are a variety of probabilities, and many more possibilities concerning Gutenberg and his work. Unfortunately, there are very few known facts. Even the place attributed to Gutenberg's most important work is suspect. At various times, historians have questioned whether Mainz, Strasbourg, or perhaps even Haarlem should be entitled to the credit of being the birthplace of Gutenberg's invention. Mainz has gotten most of the fame, because there is no doubt that the first Bible was printed there. But Strasbourg is most likely the place where Gutenberg developed his invention and fine-tuned the craft for which he is so well known.

## WAS GUTENBERG REALLY THE FIRST?

There is even a theory that one Lourens Coster of Holland beat Gutenberg to the punch. The story goes that the Dutchman, during an afternoon stroll in the local woods, occupied himself by cutting letters out of beech bark. Upon returning home, it occurred to him to set them side by side to form words and sentences. He then tried inking them and impressing them on paper for the amusement of his grandchildren. The story continues that he ultimately discarded the wood letters and replaced them with ones cast from metal. With these he printed entire books. Unfortunately, his invention was then stolen by a young German, Johann Gutenberg, who carried the idea to Mainz, where he reaped rich profits from his theft, depriving poor Coster of the cash and credit that were his due.

It is probably true that Gutenberg of Mainz invented typography, but he was uncannily successful in concealing what he was doing from just about everybody. Not once in Gutenberg's lifetime did the slightest hint of what he was working on get itself recorded in any document that has since been recovered. However, the fact that typography was

EARLY ILLUSTRATION OF A PRINTING
PRESS FROM THE *DANSE MACABRE,*
PRINTED BY MATHIAS HUS LYONS, 1499

Gutenberg's invention was common knowledge by the 15th century, and ever since then, the fact has been accepted by the general public.

The record of Gutenberg's accomplishment was apparently first put into print in 1470, by three Germans hired to set up a press at the University of Sorbonne in Paris. The statement was a simple letter of thanks written by the three men's sponsor to Gutenberg's superior, who had supplied the money to finance the novel undertaking. Thereafter, Gutenberg's name, the place, and date of his work were essentially established.

## ON THE TRAIL OF
## THE ELUSIVE GUTENBERG

Gutenberg's whereabouts can be confirmed by the trail of creditor accounts that followed him. He can be placed in Strasbourg during the years he was banished from Mainz, because his name is found on the lists of the city tax assessors and in the books of various creditors who regularly recorded his failure to make payments due. Another fortunate historical record for the student of printing history came about as a result of one of Gutenberg's financial transactions that led to legal proceedings. A large part of the legal record survived and provides some insight into the secret project of the German entrepreneur.

The trouble started shortly after the death of Andreas Dritzehen, a gentleman whose brothers found an agreement showing that Dritzehen had given money to Gutenberg. The money was given to insure his share in the profits expected from a project that he and Gutenberg had been working on. Either Gutenberg was somewhat paranoid about his project, or he was very shrewd in his business dealings (although the latter is unlikely), because his agreement with Dritzehen provided that he was under no obligation unless the venture produced a profit. It further stated that he was not liable to a partner who died before the project was completed.

Failing to establish any legal claim or to induce Gutenberg to allow them to take their brother's place in the business venture, the heirs brought suit. All they succeeded in obtaining, however, was a very small sum of money and the knowledge that Gutenberg was an expert in keeping his operations well concealed.

The court was able to determine only that Gutenberg and his various business partners were engaged in a scheme to produce a product, and that their intentions were to sell it to the many pilgrims who were to attend a great pilgrimage to Aix-la-Chapelle (Aachen). Gutenberg was to settle his accounts after the pilgrimage had assembled. Unfortunately, the bubonic plague came to Strasbourg before the pilgrims arrived. Dritzehen and many others died. The pilgrimage was canceled; the investors were left with no market for the things they had made.

The court proceedings did provide a small hint of what the partners had been working on. A determined witness testified that one partner, when forced to answer a direct question about his business, said that he was a mirror maker, a *spiegelmacher*. Nothing in this suggests anything of printing; in fact, several historians have taken this to mean that Gutenberg was indeed making mirrors prior to his work with type. If the witness had not spoken in the local dialect, but had instead used Latin, the language of the educated, then he could have said that he was making a *speculum*. If this had been the case, the end product would have been very different. A speculum was one of the most common

INITIAL "B" FROM THE LATIN
PSALTER COMPLETED AT MAINZ BY
FUST AND SCHOEFFER IN 1457

religious manuals of the time. And the *Speculum Humanae Salvationis, The Looking Glass of Salvation,* would surely be a more likely article than a hand mirror to sell to devout pilgrims visiting a shrine.

Testimony from another witness combined with the statement about the *Speculum,* gives added insight into Gutenberg's work. That other witness was one Hans Dunne, who stated that he had supplied "certain material" to Gutenberg on a speculative basis and had received, in return, payment of 100 guilders. Thus, Gutenberg had a way to pay back at least some of his debts. He was apparently producing something that could be sold for profit, and he had a way of disposing of his goods without the knowledge of his neighbors. To do this, he would need a sales agent outside Strasbourg, perhaps in Holland.

## AN ANSWER TO THE COSTER QUESTION

If Gutenberg was sending printed items to be sold at a distance, prior to his work at Mainz, and if Haarlem was the place where his secret agent lived, then the Coster story becomes much easier to explain.

If Gutenberg was exporting his goods and his secret agent lived in Haarlem (there are records of printed work being sold in Holland prior to Gutenberg's work in Mainz), then these facts could begin to explain the Coster story. While there is no documentation to prove that this was the case, there is also nothing to disprove it.

In addition, there is an obvious flaw in the Coster story as it is commonly told. This lies in the ease with which it glides from the use wood to the use of metal for printing purposes. This easy transition overlooks the most important concept of printing, which is not the mere impression of inked letters on paper, but the problem of devising a process that enables such impressions to be multiplied quickly and easily. A skilled woodcarver, in the course of a days work, might produce a cluster of letters fitting well enough together to transfer to paper an impression that would compare favorably to the work of an ordinary scribe. Meanwhile, the scribe would outproduce the woodcarver by several pages of text. The Coster theory solves only one part of the problem of printing: how to make a page of text that looks as good as that created by a scribe. Gutenberg solved this problem and a more difficult one: how to duplicate the work of the scribes speedily and economically.

Enough is known about Gutenberg to substantiate an opinion that he, like so many other creative people, was never satisfied with what he had accomplished, but that he was always trying new ideas to improve his craft and other avenues of expression. Gutenberg was not one to settle for what he had achieved and comfortably exploit profits from a single work. Once he had produced one piece successfully, he most likely went on to produce other products. Calendars, medical handbooks, and booklets of poems are all part of the printing historians have found, and these could very well predate the best known work of the Mainz printer.

## LINKS TO THE BIBLE TYPE

One set of type can be clearly traced as a direct predecessor to that used in the *42-Line Gutenberg Bible.* This was a typeface used to set a calendar and a 15th-century version of an elementary grammar book. This same type has been proven to almost certainly be related to those used for the *36-Line Bible,* which some historians also attribute to Gutenberg. Logic would normally lead us to conclude that a book set in large, crude type (such as in the *36-Line Bible*) would precede one set in much more refined cuttings. The calendar, because of the dates it covers, helps to place the earlier type in its correct historical time slot. There is, however, some controversy regarding the *36-Line* types. It seems that they were also used to set a Bible that postdates Gutenberg's first

Bible. An answer to this apparent mystery is that Gutenberg created the bigger and less refined type to set the calendar, but that the type fell into the hands of others when he discarded it after developing better fonts. When Gutenberg produced the *42-Line Bible,* the printers in possession of the older type used it to set a copy of his work.

Shortly after the Dritzehen incident, Gutenberg left Strasbourg. Apparently he was no longer able to find fresh capital to finance his scheme. The last mention of Gutenberg in Strasbourg appears in the tax registers of March 1444, when he paid an excise duty on the contents of his wine cellar, which was, we are told, always well stocked in spite of his financial misfortunes.

## GUTENBERG DISAPPEARS

Four years of Gutenberg's life—from the time he left Strasbourg until he settled once again in Mainz—are entirely unaccounted for. The next official record of Gutenberg's whereabouts appears in the Mainz town record of October 1448. The record shows that, once again, Gutenberg was a borrower. But by this time his credit was so impaired that he had to find a co-signer for the loan, even though the note was for a comparatively small amount of money. Yet Gutenberg's powers of persuasion were far from exhausted. The following year he borrowed again. This time he entered into his famous association with another citizen of Mainz, the lawyer Johann Fust.

In about 1450, Gutenberg received a loan from Fust for 800 guilders, carrying an interest of 6 percent. The money was to be used to complete the work on a printing press and begin the work of producing a product to be sold for profit. The press was held as collateral. After some time, it became apparent that the original 800 guilders was not enough and Gutenberg applied for a second loan. Fust declined blind support but offered instead to advance Gutenberg 800 guilders on the condition of being taken on as a full part-

ner in the business venture. Gutenberg agreed, and resumed his efforts. The result was the legendary *42-Line Gutenberg Bible.*

## DISSECTING THE 42-LINE BIBLE

The *42-Line Bible* is not as scarce as many would think. There are still approximately 40 copies left in various places around the world. As a result, historians have been able to examine the book in minute detail and have made a curious discovery.

In about half of the copies, all the pages were set in the famous 42-line type. But in other books, apparently other sizes of type were used. In these, the first nine pages have only 40 lines per page, and the tenth page has 41 lines: a typographic mystery.

Seeking an explanation, typographic historians and scientific bibliographers examined those early pages with microscopes and enlarging cameras. Their sophisticated equipment enabled them to detect, on the tops and bottoms of some letters in the 41-line columns, and on the next few 42-line pages, very faint but unmistakable blurs. When enlarged, these were shown to be parallel lines. This is all the historians found, but it was all they needed to prove that the original 40-line type was filed down to enable more lines to be set on a page. The result was the 42-line type used to set Gutenberg's most famous Bible.

Gutenberg, with the help of Fust's money, designed a new type, each letter about a millimeter shorter than the 36-line types used to set the calendar and the earlier Bible. This new type was cast on the same size of metal base (or body) as the previous type. A supply of this new type was cast, and Gutenberg's workers went about setting copy from a manuscript Bible. When the first few pages were set and printed, Gutenberg looked at the results but apparently wasn't pleased with what he saw. He decided that the line space could be reduced. This was probably more for economic, rather than es-

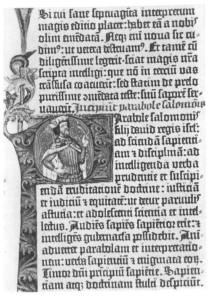

ILLUMINATED INITIAL DEPICTING KING SOLOMON FROM *PROVERBS* IN THE 42-LINE BIBLE

A ROMANTICIZED PAINTING OF JOHANN GUTENBERG SHOWING A PRESS PROOF OF HIS 42-LINE BIBLE. ARTIST UNKNOWN. CULVER PICTURES.

thetic, reasons (paper was even more expensive in the 15th century than now). Nevertheless, he was the boss, and this boss was used to getting his way.

To bring the printed lines closer together, Gutenberg had his workers file a little metal off the tops and bottoms of the type. In doing so, every once in a while the file touched the top or bottom of the letter, leaving the telltale lines. This first experiment resulted in the 41-line page. Deciding that even a little more space could be saved, Gutenberg repeated the process. Finally, a 42-line page was achieved, and new type was cast to this smaller point body. The result netted Gutenberg with the Bible we are familiar with today—and an approximate 5 percent saving in paper consumption.

## THE BEGINNING OF THE END

Unfortunately, Gutenberg's experimentation also probably led to the event that caused Fust to foreclose on his loans. The question that has been raised by many is, if Gutenberg was so close to finishing the project, why did Fust call in his note? Surely, it would have been paid if Gutenberg had been allowed to finish his work. In addition, Fust would have shared in the profits.

The answer? It is entirely possible that Fust decided that the work would be delayed more frequently, and unnecessarily, if Gutenberg continued to have new ideas and stopped the presses each time he thought of additional changes. This probably led the financier to insist that the inventor give up direct control of the project, and that someone with fewer ideas, and more executive ability, take the helm. That someone was Fust's son-in-law, Peter Schoeffer.

Fust and Schoeffer did, in fact, take control of the Bible very near the end of the project. Unfortunately, this left no place in the business for Gutenberg. As a result, Fust came to the same decision that many pragmatic businessmen would have reached: He laid Gutenberg off. With no

job, no type, and no printing press, Gutenberg was a beaten man—almost.

## NEW MONEY, NEW HOPE, NEW PROJECTS

After a short hiatus, presumably to rally his spirits, Gutenberg once again began to look for financial support. And once again he found a patron. This time it was Dr. Conrad Homery, who on February 26, 1468, formally acknowledged return from the estate of the late Johann Gutenberg of what appears to be the complete equipment for a press, which was the doctor's property. Evidently, some time after Gutenberg left his former place of employment, Homery had supplied him with the means for resuming his labors. This enabled Gutenberg to complete his last, and perhaps some of his most important, work as an inventor and printer. Between the time he parted company with Fust and his death, one large volume and three small tracts were printed in Mainz which are also attributed to Gutenberg. Historians have assigned these to Gutenberg because there was nobody else to claim them. But additionally, and more importantly, phrases in the colophon of the larger work, *The Catholicon,* were almost certainly written by Gutenberg himself.

## THE BIG BOOK WITH THE LITTLE TYPE

The *Catholicon of Johannes Balbus* was an immense Latin dictionary and encyclopedia of sorts. It was the forerunner of similar catch-alls of universal knowledge. These great-grandparents of the home encyclopedia were published successfully by enterprising printers for many years after Gutenberg.

The *Catholicon* introduced a new and profitable business venture to the first printers: that of informative publications intended for sale to the public. More significant than either the subject or its huge size, however, is the type with which the *Catholicon* was printed. This type was about one-third the size of that used in the *42-Line Bible,* and is approximately the size that the general public, from that day to the present, have found most satisfactory for reading. Its introduction involved much more than the designing and cutting of smaller letters. Before type of this size could be cast, the molds had to be improved dramatically. Much smaller metal bodies—some of them as thin as the paper then in use—had to be cast without losing the face of the narrowest letters. This accomplishment was a crowning triumph of the German inventor's mechanical skill and ingenuity.

Gutenberg's *Catholicon* was not, however, the earliest dated publication to appear printed in such small type. A few months earlier, Fust and Schoeffer brought out a treatise on liturgical practice, *Rationale Divinorum Officiorum,* by Guillelmus Durandus, in which they also used small type. The text type for this book was about the same size as that of the *Catholicon.* But to place this book be-

fore Gutenberg's work just because it is dated earlier would probably not be a fair conclusion. The main reason the Fust and Schoeffer book did not predate Gutenberg's *Catholicon* is that the Fust/Schoeffer publication is less than half the size of the *Catholicon,* 320 pages compared to the latter's 750. What likely took place is that the wealthy, well-equipped printing office of Fust and Schoeffer learned that Gutenberg had come up with another new idea (trade secrets were difficult to maintain in the 15th century) and directed their efforts to the development of a similar size of type. With their new type, they produced a book that was adapted to their special clientele, consisting largely of churchmen, and issued it before Gutenberg's book was complete.

## WHO WAS JOHANN GUTENBERG?

Very little is actually known about the life of Johann Gutenberg. Most representations of him, including the one in this

PORTIONS OF *THE ANNUNCIATION* FROM THE 42-LINE AND 36-LINE BIBLE

chapter, derive from an engraving made in 1584. In it he is pictured as an elderly man in a fur cap, a forked beard, and a rather vacant expression. (The "vacant expression" is perhaps due to the entire uselessness, for typographical purposes, of the die engraved with the first four letters of the alphabet which he holds in his left hand.) This is obviously a work of pure fancy, if only because Gutenberg, as a patrician and a member of an archepiscopal household, would have been clean-shaven.

Johann Gutenberg belonged to the family of Gensfleisch, patrician clan of Mainz, at the confluence of the Rhine and Main rivers. Mainz was the seat of an archbishop and a city of considerable importance in the 15th century. His full name was Johann Gensfleisch zur Laden, but apparently he was content to be known as Gutenberg, after the house in which his family lived. The exact date of Gutenberg's birth is unknown, but he was probably born between 1394 and 1399. His death is, however, recorded as February 3, 1468.

Mainz was well reputed for the number and skill of its workers in precious metals. Many members of the Gensfleisch clan, including Johann's father, were associated with the archepiscopal mint. Gutenberg, therefore, had an early familiarity with the goldsmith's craft. This, more than likely, proved to be an advantage in the early development of his invention.

In 1411, Gutenberg's father was driven out of Mainz into temporary exile. When, in 1428, the trade guilds succeeded in stripping the patricians of their civic privileges, young Johann also left Mainz. He settled at Strasbourg, where he began his first experimenting with printing and movable type.

Gutenberg lived in Strasbourg for more than 20 years. He even preferred to stay there after amnesty provided him the opportunity to return to his homeland. It was eventually financial pressure, rather than homesickness, that led Gutenberg to return to his native city.

Two events recorded in Strasbourg provide a glimpse into Gutenberg's personality: one when he was sued for breach of promise of marriage, and the other for slander. The woman in the breach of promise suit was unsuccessful in forcing Gutenberg's hand, and he remained unmarried for the rest of his life. One witness to the breach of promise case was a shoemaker who provided evidence against Gutenberg. Apparently hot-tempered, Gutenberg publicly derided the man, calling him "a poor creature, leading a life of lies and deceit." As a result, the shoemaker sued Gutenberg—and won. The result cost Gutenberg 15 guilders in damages.

## GUTENBERG'S KNOWN CONTRIBUTIONS

Gutenberg's greatest contribution may well be that his printing reached a state of technical efficiency that was not surpassed until the beginning of the 19th century. Punch-cutting, matrix-fitting, typecasting, composing, and printing remained, for more than three centuries, very much as they had been in Gutenberg's time. In fact, until the end of the 18th century, Gutenberg's original design was still regarded as the "common" press.

While Gutenberg did not invent most of the devices for which he is given credit, his achievement lies in the scientific synthesis of them into an economical, practical product. The adjustable mold, which Gutenberg did invent, enabled one model produced by a designer to be replicated many thousands of times. It also established the principle, three centuries before it was generally adopted by industry, of the theory of interchangeable parts —the basis of all modern mass-produced products.

Gutenberg may have been a poor businessperson; he may even have been a charlatan. Perhaps he didn't invent many of the things for which he is generally given credit. But there is no disputing that he gave us the craft of printing, the art of typeface design, and as a result, the ability to communicate in a manner that is exceptionally utilitarian and yet supremely elegant.

# William Caxton

## 1421–1491

Typographic history is peppered with egos. No one would ever describe Johann Gutenberg, Aldus Manitius, Giambattista Bodoni, or Stanley Morison, as being shrinking violets. These were passionate men, who, through their strength of will and remarkable talent, had extraordinary influence on the shaping of our typographic standards and tradition.

As with all things typographic, however, there are exceptions. England's first printer, and certainly one of its most important, was a simple and exceptionally unegotistical person. For much of his life, William Caxton was a merchant. For all of his life, he suffered from a world-class inferiority complex. To further separate Caxton from the norm, he was not a talented type designer or even a particularly skilled typographer. And yet this unassuming and well-meaning merchant paved the way for the English renaissance.

Textbooks credit Caxton with printing the first books in England. He would deserve recognition even if this had been his only contribution to history. But William Caxton did much more.

## Not Just Type

Not only did Caxton print the first English book and introduce the art of printing to England, he also did as much as anyone has ever done to establish the English language as a vehicle for literary expression. At a critical period, when English literature was at a low point, and when the spoken language of England was a hodgepodge of regional dialects, he introduced the printing press to his homeland. By determining that the press should produce only works in the English language, Caxton performed a service of inestimable literary value to English-speaking people.

Caxton accomplished all of this after he was well into his fifties.

Caxton returned to London in the late autumn of 1476, after spending more than 35 years representing British commercial interests on the European conti-nent. He began his career as a merchant, but by his retirement he had become a diplomat entrusted with the management of treaties that vitally affected the prosperity of England's foreign commerce.

After such a long and successful career, most people would be ready to retire, and Caxton was no exception.

But then something happened that compelled him to pursue what was to become a consuming passion that gave him a new career and added new meaning to his life.

## Beginnings of the Second Career

Late in his tenure as a trade diplomat, Caxton had begun translating a piece of French literature into English—mostly, he said, to forestall idleness. He had been successful at negotiating treaties, improving trade relations, and creating a smoothly running European business machine for the British government. Toward the end of his career (because of earlier successes) Caxton simply had little to do.

In the spring of 1469, Caxton began to translate a popular French tale into English. After writing 40 or 50 pages of the translation, however, Caxton's self-imposed task began to lose its novelty. After 60 pages he set the work aside. He found that his new hobby wasn't fun; in fact, it was downright difficult.

Some time after the attempt at translating, Caxton completed the process of retirement from business and entered the service of the Duchess of Burgundy as sort of a semi-retired advisor. One day, while in conversation with his new employer, Caxton happened to mention his unfinished translation. Immediately the duchess demanded to see his work, for in addition to being Caxton's employer, she was also a patron of the arts. The opportunity to see important, popular literature translated into her native language intrigued and excited the duchess.

*THE BOOK OF CHESS*, PRINTED IN 1480, WAS THE FIRST ENGLISH LANGUAGE BOOK
TO USE WOODCUTS EXTENSIVELY. THE HULTON PICTURE COMPANY.

## NEW RESPONSIBILITIES

After seeing Caxton's initial work, the duchess didn't hesitate to ask Caxton to take up the project again, and although reluctant to do so, he was more reluctant to incur the duchess's displeasure. Despite his earlier accomplishments, Caxton still regarded himself as a simple merchant and was uncomfortable in his first efforts as a translator. The Duchess of Burgundy was, however, exceptionally persuasive. Although unable to rid Caxton of his insecurity, she did enable him to cope with it—or at least to continue his work in spite of it. As a result of the duchess's encouragement, Caxton later wrote that he, "forthwith went and labored in the said translation after my simple and poor cunning, all so might as I can, following mine author, meekly beseeching the bounteous highness of my said lady that of her benevolence list to accept and take —this simple and rude work."

Caxton loved literature but had long been deeply disturbed by the lack of refinement and standards of his own language. Although he was quite qualified to take on the task, he had previously lacked the self-confidence to undertake it until he was forced to do so by the duchess. Caxton probably felt that his work was more akin to a penance than a mission. He wished to please his sophisticated patron but suffered under the belief that he was neither a good translator nor a good linguist. It was only relentless determination that enabled him to succeed. One can easily imagine Caxton working far into the night, bent over his manuscripts working diligently, but without enjoyment. His failed attempt at a simple hobby had come back to haunt him.

## THE REAL GOAL

Caxton's translations were, in fact, only a painful means to a much more satisfying end result. He persevered with them only because ultimately he wanted to print books. Early on, in the process of carrying out the duchess's wishes, Caxton realized that there was, perhaps, a more fulfilling opportunity available to him as a by-product of the completed translations. Duplicating copies of his work through the new technology of printing became Caxton's goal; the translations were only the means to that end. Various reasons have been proposed for Caxton's opening a printing business. Some feel that he foresaw the revolutionary possibilities of this new technology. Others, however, contended that he desperately wanted to see books produced in the English language. Others believe that, as a merchant, he saw the tremendous commercial possibilities of acquiring a virtual monopoly for printing books in his homeland. The truth probably is that his motives were a combination of all these things. Throughout all his work, however, Caxton was passionately committed to bringing order to the English language.

Caxton's deeply felt appreciation of good language is clear from his many references to his own efforts to improve his own vocabulasry. Born, as he acknowledges in his first publication, in a part of England where, "I doubt not is spoken as broad and rude English as in any place in England," and living for most of his professional life in linguistically sophisticated countries, Caxton was naturally self-conscious about the lack of elegance in his own use of language. His everyday speech was probably a conglomerate of many northern European languages commingled with some classroom Latin.

He writes, "I confess me not learned nor knowing the arte of rethoryke, ne of suche gaye termes as how be sayed in these dayes and used." Throughout his work he continually refers to his feelings of inadequacy and lack of sophistication in matters of language. Caxton persevered for the rest of his life, producing translation after translation, to be printed at his press. Apparently, he was also always ready for a discussion of the minutiae of literary usage. All this makes England's first printer a man of great conviction who was able to overcome tremendous feelings of inadequacy, or a man who displayed false modesty. Perhaps Caxton was both.

## THE START

Born about 1422 in Kent, England, Caxton began his professional career after serving as an apprentice to one of the wealthiest and most successful London merchants of that time. Caxton's father was a well-to-do tenant farmer who also engaged in the cloth trade. It was through his father's position that Caxton obtained this important and very influential apprenticeship.

Caxton began his training at age 14, for Robert Large, a prominent member of the Mercers Company, an organization of merchants who dealt in textile fabrics, especially velvet and silk. A year after the young Caxton entered his household, Large became Lord Mayor of London, an office that added further prominence to his position and provided his apprentice with additional opportunities to learn the politics of business—and the business of politics.

## AN AMBITIOUS APPRENTICE

Caxton's master and patron unfortunately died after Caxton had completed only three years of his stewardship. However, the apprentice was not forgotten in Large's will, which bequeathed 20 marks to young Caxton. Shortly after, Caxton left his homeland and traveled to Burgundy, where English cloth merchants had their most active European business connections.

He prospered in Burgundy, and by 1449 he had become sufficiently wealthy to be accepted as a surety for another resident English merchant. But the man left Burgundy without attending to his obligations, leaving Caxton to pay the outstanding debt. The good news is that this was apparently the only unfavorable incident in an otherwise very successful business career.

Caxton was eventually made Governor of the English Nation, the Company of Merchant Adventurers resident at Bruges. The post was very much akin to that of consul in the present-day diplomatic service, and one at which Caxton also was exceptionally successful. Caxton's entire career was a model of success and prosperity.

During this time Caxton's interest in the English language increased. He became more aware of its shortcomings and fragility. Essentially a patchwork of dialects with no written foundation to maintain stability, the English language that Caxton knew was far less developed than many of the other languages of continental Europe. As Caxton's concern increased, so did his frustration, because he retained a steadfast belief that he had little capability to bring order and strength to his native tongue.

## An Honest Assessment

Besides his feelings of inadequacy as a linguist, Caxton did not consider himself to be a particularly accomplished printer or typographer. Here, however, there is no false modesty. Many of the early surviving books and other printed material which came from Caxton's press show clearly that England's first typographer was not interested in the development of typesetting as an art form. He issued nothing that would compare favorably with the better work of his contemporaries on the European continent. In addition, Caxton's apparent slight regard for typographic quality cannot be attributed to lack of awareness. The work of French, German, and Dutch printers was certainly available to Caxton, and he probably saw their work on many occasions. In spite of this, for the first several years that his press produced books, his products were almost crude by continental standards. The typefaces were coarse copies of northern European fonts, his printing

quality was clearly less than optimal, and many of his earlier books even lacked signatures, title pages, or illustrations.

Why didn't Caxton seek to improve his craft? Why didn't he strive to equal the work of his European contemporaries? Because his true mission, the driving force behind his work, was not the design and printing of books, but the books themselves. His goal was to print as many books as he could and to make those books easy to read and accessible to a wide audience. Caxton was not producing works of art, he was trying to build an English literary tradition.

After Caxton's press had been in business for a little more than five years, however, the shop's output changed noticeably. Books began to have signatures, illustrations began to appear, and the quality of the typography improved.

What had caused the change? Competition. About this time, a rival printing shop opened just a short distance away from Caxton's. In an attempt to counter his competition, Caxton hired a new foreman and resigned from the position of chief typographer. The good news about Caxton's new employee is that he was relocated from continental Europe and was familiar with the practices and standards of printing in France and Germany. The new foreman not only proved instrumental in improving the work produced at Caxton's press, he also carried on the business of the press for 45 years after Caxton's death. Thus, Jan van Wynkyn de Worde (or as he is commonly known: Wynkyn de Worde), an Alsace-born expatriate, became England's first typographer.

## The Mysterious Art

Nobody is really quite sure where Caxton learned the new art of printing, and Caxton himself seems to have gone out of his way to keep this information secret. Numerous stories have been told, however —some quite fanciful—that attempt to explain the circumstances of Caxton's printing education. One typographic folk tale suggests that King Henry VI commissioned Caxton and another man to sneak into Holland and learn the Dutch secrets of printing. The two men supposedly were involved in high-level espionage, complete with clandestine meetings, disguises, hush money, and the abduction of a trained printer. But most historians believe that Caxton learned his craft in Cologne. This is supported by a statement made by Wynkyn de Worde, in the prologue of a book published shortly after Caxton's death.

"And also of your charyte call to remberance
The soule of William Caxton first prynter of this boke
I laten tonge at Coleyn hymself to avavnce
That every well disposyd man may ther on-loke"

Why Caxton went to Cologne, however, is a part of the story that historians have been unable to unravel. Some believe that the answer could be as simple as that he had already planned to travel to Cologne on holiday when he was asked by the Duchess of Burgundy to finish his first translation. It could also have been that Caxton, being a good businessman, saw the potential value of his translations, especially if they could be sold to other royalty—instead of just the Duchess of Burgundy. By the time Caxton had begun his work for the Duchess, printing had established itself as a hot new technology in Europe, and Cologne, if not the "Silicon Valley" of this new technology, was certainly closely akin to it. If the latter had been Caxton's plan, then it was successful, because British royalty did, in fact, become the primary customers for Caxton's work after he set up business in England.

## THE REAL PRODUCT

The first book Caxton published, and the first book printed in the English language, was the translation requested by the Duchess. This was a small folio of 351 leaves, the first of which, containing Caxton's *Prologue,* was printed in red. Some historians date this volume to 1471, the year the *Prologue* states that the translation was finished. But those who are more familiar with the difficulty of using early type fonts and printing equipment believe that three to four years could easily have been consumed in producing this effort.

Caxton's first book was followed by *The Game and Play of Chess Moralised.* This was a translation of a popular French book that likened the game of chess to life itself. Caxton was fascinated by the comparison and the lessons it posed. He also decided that if he liked the book, then his fellow Englishmen should also be exposed to both the game and the book.

These first two books and one other were printed while Caxton lived in Bruges, on the continent of Europe. Then, in the autumn of 1476, Caxton returned to England after nearly 30 years of absence, to set up a printing business in the Almonry of Westminster Abbey.

In the 14 years that Caxton operated his business, he printed more than 18,000 pages, mostly of folio size, and nearly 80 books. As time passed, Caxton became less of a typographer and printer and more of an overseer. His three main assistants—Wynkyn de Worde, Richard Pynson, and Robert Copland—increasingly undertook the tasks of type founding, typesetting, and printing, giving Caxton more time to concentrate on his translations.

While working in England, Caxton translated 21 works from Latin, French, and Dutch literature. All but one of these were printed by him, and three of them were also brought out as second editions. By current standards, 21 translations may not seem like a major effort, but it was a substantial literary labor in the late 15th century. Most of the books were about 250 pages long, or a total of approximately 2,850,000 words. This means that Caxton translated 400 words a day for 240 days a year during the 25 years after he retired from active life in the world of public affairs.

## ANOTHER FIRST

Because Caxton was England's first printer, and because being a printer in the 15th century meant, for the most part, designing and founding your own type, Caxton was also England's first type founder. During the 27 years of his involvement in printing, he developed and used eight typefaces.

For his first font, Caxton persuaded a noted Flemish calligrapher to change his profession to that of typeface designer. The end result is generally a somewhat crude and awkward typeface, but a design that was consistent with Flemish handwriting of the time. Caxton used this type only for the first three books he published in Bruges and did not bring it with him to England. Apparently, Caxton did such a good job of persuading his type designer to switch careers that the former calligrapher kept that type and used it to start his own printing business in Bruges.

Caxton's second typeface, unimaginatively called Type 2 by historians, was designed and cast in England and is generally classified as a Flemish *Batarda* style. It is patterned after a German gothic style but is more cursive. Of the eight Caxton types, three are of this *Batarda* style. The others are more in keeping with the angular and pointed *Black Letter* types of northern Germany. One of these is generally considered to be the ancestor of the "Old English" types that are still used today.

## RED PALE ADVERTISING

Not only was Caxton England's first printer, type designer, and type founder, he also established England's first advertising agency. Upon his return to England, he opened his printing business at the "Sign of the Red Pale." However, few people in England knew about the new craft of printing, and fewer still knew about Caxton's recently opened business. Being an intelligent businessperson, he used his new medium to tell people about his products and services. Thus, the first English advertising handbill was printed. It was followed by others that periodically advertised the work of his new printing business at the Sign of the Red Pale.

When William Caxton died in 1491, he had completed a widely varied career. He had contributed to the commercial prosperity of 15th-century England, he had introduced both printing and type founding into England, and he had provided English readers with some of the best foreign and English literature. Although his commercial exploits were not inconsequential, by far Caxton's greatest contribution was to the English language. His efforts increased English-speaking people's awareness of the poetry and literature of their time and paved the way for generations of great English writers to follow. Surely there might have been no English Renaissance had it not been for the likes of William Caxton.

# Aldus Manutius

1450–1515

It's an old problem: who owns the final product of a joint creative product? Is it the person responsible for the initial creative idea? The one who transformed that idea into a reality? Or the person who marketed the product and established its value?

Aldus Manutius and Francesco Griffo da Bologna faced this problem together. The two men formed a creative team that produced some of the communication industry's most important and influential typeface designs. As in many close and intensely creative relationships, however, the two also quarreled and eventually parted over the issue of product ownership.

## CREATIVE TEAM SPLITS UP

The break in the affiliation between Griffo and Manutius did not occur because of a personality clash, but because of a rapidly changing commercial environment. At the time they worked, the typographic industry was evolving from the pioneer age, when one person usually directed every stage of the type design process to a more regulated and structured environment. The organized and somewhat reliable industry of Garamond and Plantin, when a number of recognized and skilled punch cutters supplied the needs of established clientele, still lay in the future. Aldus and Griffo fell between the two extremes, of one person entrepreneurial shops and multi-employee printing business, and the lack of an established work pattern eventually caused their split.

Aldus was an entrepreneur, and his break with Griffo resulted from his trying to ensure the future of his company and protect its assets. The clumsy system of press-privilege popular in 15th-century Italy sought only to protect the interests of the investor, and that always meant the printer or publisher. Aldus was both. So when he tried to protect his company's substantial investment with a privilege that outlawed all imitation of his type styles, he effectively, though perhaps un-

intentionally, prevented Griffo from selling his best and most popular designs to other printers. It is no wonder, then, that the two men quarreled. There is no doubt that Griffo was a creative genius, and that without his type designs Aldus's accomplishments would not have been nearly so important. However, Aldus created the environment that made Griffo's work possible and the conditions that made his typeface designs necessary.

## A GREAT SCHOLAR-PRINTER

Next to Gutenberg, Aldus was perhaps the most important printer of the Renaissance and the first of many great scholar-printers. A successful publisher and businessman, Aldus produced some of the most beautiful and technically accurate books of the 15th century. The Aldine roman, the most popular type style of its time and the model for hundreds of other designs, was but one of his contributions to typography. The portable book and italic type faces are both Aldus innovations. Before Aldus's time, all books had been much larger, and italics were used only as a writing style. Few have contributed as much or as widely to enrich our typographic heritage as did Aldus Manutius.

To accomplish his many goals, Aldus gathered some of the most creative and talented members of the European printing and publishing community. People like Erasmus, the famous Dutch philosopher, were commonly drawn to his shop. Technicians and laborers were recruited with offers promising high pay and exciting projects. Aldus went to extreme lengths to surround himself with the brightest and the best. It is therefore a little odd that he showed very little understanding of, or good will toward, those who worked so hard for him. Aldus rarely mentioned his co-workers or staff in any of his writings, even though they worked and lived on his property. What little is written about them is not laudatory. In the preface to one of his books, he once referred to his workers as his

```
VNII IVVENALIS AQVINA
TIS SATYRA PRIMA.

            EMPER EGO AVDITOR
            tantùm? nunquàm ne reponam
   S        V exatus toties raua theseide
            Codri?
            I mpune ergo mihi recitauerit ille
            togatas?
H ic elegos? impune diem consumpserit ingens
I elephus? aut summi plena iam margine libri
S criptus, et in tergo nec dum finitus, Orestes?
N ota magis nulli domus est sua, quam mihi lucus
M artis, et æoliis uicinum rupibus antrum
V ulcani. Quid agant uenti, quas torqueat umbras
A eacus, unde alius furtiuæ deuehat aurum
P elliculæ, quantas iaculetur Monychus ornos,
F rontonis platani, conuulsáq; marmora clamant
S emper, et assiduo ruptæ lectore columnæ.
E xpectes eadem a summo, minimóq; poeta.
E t nos ergo manum ferulæ subduximus, et nos
C onsilium dedimus Syllæ, priuatus ut altum
D ormiret. stulta est clementia, cum tot ubique
V atibus occurras, perituræ parcere chartæ.
C ur tamen hoc libeat potius decurrere campo,
```

ALDUS' ITALIC, VENICE 1501, CUT
BY FRANCESCO GRIFFO

"damned runaway slaves," and in another piece he complained that "my hired men and workers have conspired against me in my own house . . . but with the help of God I smashed them that they all thoroughly regret their treachery." Whether is was with the help of God or that of his principal partner, a member of Italian royalty, it is well recorded that Aldus dealt harshly and remorselessly with those who stood in his way. In personal and business matters, it is recorded that Aldus was capable of extraordinary insensitivity and malice.

## INVENTION OF THE SMALL BOOK

Many historians tell us that Aldus first invented small books. He did not. Some say that his work with small publications grew out of an altruistic drive to supply learned text to the masses. This also is a misconception. Aldus was not altruistic; he was a shrewd and creative businessman driven by goals more pragmatic than benevolent.

Small books were printed before Aldus's time, but the majority of printed material was large—the kind intended for libraries, bookstands, and oral reading. When Aldus began his work, the printing industry was less than 50 years old and still bound by the traditions of scribes and illuminated manuscripts. Small books, or octavos (made from single sheets folded three times, each sheet forming eight leaves, or sixteen pages about 6 × 9 inches), were published before Aldus's time. As early as 1470, more than 30 years before Aldus's first work, Nicholas Jenson had printed some small religious texts. There had been still others, but one very important aspect separates those earlier books from Aldus's small texts: All the previous editions were of a religious or devotional nature. Prayer was considered the only occasion which required an individual to carry a book on one's person. The scholar was expected to read from a large book sitting on a lectern. Aldus's originality lay in applying what had previously been a specialized book form to a new and wider field. Aldus was a marketer, not a humanitarian.

A story has evolved that Aldus created the small book for those who could not otherwise afford to purchase literature. Because smaller books cost less to produce, the reduced costs were thus passed along to the consumer. However, Aldus never stated that his books were inexpensive. He often said that they were beautiful, that they were technically perfect, and that they were convenient, but never that they were inexpensive or meant for a mass audience. It has been suggested that Aldus would probably "writhe in his grave" if he knew that many printing scholars credit him as being the originator of the paperback.

Aldus worked for the benefit of the wealthy and the successful. His octavos were intended for busy people of worldly affairs—those who crisscrossed 15th- and 16th-century Europe on the errands of nobility and the business of state. Aldus created his small books for the secular intellectuals of Renaissance Europe, for the people who filled the growing

ALDUS MANUTIUS' TRADEMARK

POLIPHILO INCOMINCIA IL SECONDO LIBRO DI
LA SVA HYPNEROTOMACHIA. NEL QVALE PO-
LIA ET LVI DISERTABONDI, IN QVALE MODO ET
VARIO CASO NARRANO INTERCALARIAMEN-
TE IL SVO INAMORAMENTO.

NARRA QVIVI LA DIVA POLIA LA NOBILE ET
ANTIQVA ORIGINE SVA, ET COMO PER LI PREDE
CESSORI SVI TRIVISIO FVE EDIFICATO. ET DI QVEL
LA GENTE LELIA ORIVNDA. ET PER QVALE MO-
DO DISAVEDVTA ET INSCIA DISCONCIAMENTE
SE INAMORO E DI LEI IL SVO DILECTO POLIPHILO.

PAGE OF *HYPNEROIOMACHIA
POLIPHILI:* ALDUS, VENICE, 1499

number of universities to prepare for employment as government officials and public servants. These were the people of the educational revolution in 16th-century Europe.

Even though Aldus's small books were not intended to expand the knowledge of the masses, it still remains that they were a vital development in the emancipation of the uneducated. The "fairy tale" of books for everybody may not be true, but the fact of his small books' importance, worth, and influence certainly is. With this contribution alone, Aldus could be remembered and revered. He made reading convenient and learning "user friendly." He set a precedent for personal books of high caliber. And he created texts that were portable yet possessing all the beauty and quality of the larger, library editions.

## INVENTION OF ITALIC TYPE

Another typographic tale concerns Aldus's invention of italic type. Whether true or not, the story is told that Aldus paid Griffo to develop a space-saving cursive type for his small books. It is said that Aldus's goal was to cut paper costs and thus make his publications less expensive. Then, as now, paper was expensive, but saving paper was not Aldus's goal in creating italic type.

Early 16th-century printers spoke of "writing" a typeset page as if it were a letter to a friend. As this somewhat unusual terminology, by today's standards, implies, the typeface provided a much closer link between printer and reader than it does today. Certain styles of type were reserved for specific groups of readers. Aldus was trying less to save space than to appeal to the educated, worldly, and wealthy.

Aldus's italic type evolved from a popular writing style used by the educated. Its heritage can be traced back to Niccolo de Niccoli, an Italian scholar of the early 15th century. De Niccoli started to oblique and add flourish to his letters when "he wished to write in a faster,

more relaxed fashion than usual." By midcentury other scholars began to imitate his writing style, and by the late 1400s, italic became the official writing style of the learned and of the professional scribes of southern Italy. In fact, the style came to be called *cancellaresca* because of the large volume of work produced in this type for the city chancelleries.

The cursive style of writing had been developed by the same scholars and learned government officials for whom Aldus created his books. In adapting the style to print, he and Griffo were making their books more appealing to their intended audience. Today, we would call this tactic creative marketing. What is important is that Aldus took an exclusive writing style—almost an art form—and turned it into a typeface, a product that would appeal to, as well as benefit, a growing and eager audience.

## PROTECTING THE INVESTMENT

Like any other astute businessperson, Aldus was very aware of the potential value of his product. In an effort to defend his exclusive right to its use, he sought the first known patent privileges for a type style. This was breaking new ground. Previously, only specific book titles were protected, but Aldus had friends in high places and in 1502, the Venetian senate granted his italics official protection. Still unsatisfied, Aldus sought additional, and what he believed was maximum, security from theft. He even had his types protected by papal decree. Aldus was one of the best protected publishers and type developers of his time, and perhaps of all time.

Unfortunately, his efforts were to little avail. Aldus's italics were copied almost immediately. First they were copied by Griffo, who felt that the design was, after all, his own; later they were copied by contemporary Italian and French printers. The Italians called the design "Aldino," at least referring to its originator. Others called it "italic," after Italy. When he could, Aldus fought those who copied his design—some through legal means; others through aggressive business tactics.

Aldus was swift and ruthless. Unfortunately, he was also for the most part, unsuccessful. His italic type became the model for generations of cursive designs. Aldus gave the typographic community one of its most important and beautiful tools, but not entirely willingly.

For all Aldus's efforts to protect his italic font, he never sought to protect any of his roman fonts. Because he did not actively promote the books he set in these designs, it can be gathered that he cared little for them.

Perhaps he cared so little because, in 15th-century Italy, important works were seldom set in roman type. Most scholarly work was set in Greek. (Aldus was very proud and protective of his Greek type.)

He used his roman types seldom, and only for pieces sponsored by wealthy clients or academic friends. As a consequence, many of his roman types were considered poorly designed—all but one.

In February 1496, Aldus published a rather insignificant essay by the Italian scholar Pietro Bembo. The type used for the text became instantly popular. So famous did it become that it influenced typeface design for generations. Posterity has come to regard the Bembo type as Aldus's and Griffo's masterpiece.

## A WATERSHED DESIGN

The design was lighter and more harmonious in weight than earlier romans. Text that was set in Bembo type was inviting and easy to read. The basic design was further enhanced by the introduction, three years later, of a font of corresponding capital letters. (The Bembo roman was initially produced as only a lowercase font with capitals pulled from other faces.) The capitals are not quite as tall as the ascenders and they blend exceptionally well with the lowercase. Bembo has a more pronounced weight than previous romans; it is more even in color; and the serifs are lighter and more delicate. Aldus's and Griffo's original Bembo design looks somewhat like the romans used today.

This face, which was modestly launched in a 60-page favor to a friend and became eminently popular in Italy, soon found its way to France. The design came to the attention of Garamond, the famous French type founder, and through his efforts to duplicate it the design eventually spread its influence to Germany, Holland, and the rest of Europe. The Aldine roman was to become the foundation of new typeface designs for hundreds of years.

Aldus entered printing rather late in life—after age 40. There is much conjecture among type scholars as to why Aldus left a life of comparative ease as a successful scholar with a noble constituency for a life of toil, labor, and the financial uncertainty of establishing a printing press and publishing business.

## A TRUE RENAISSANCE MAN

Little is said of Aldus in history books, except those dealing with the specialized fields of Venetian or Italian life in the 15th and 16th centuries. Yet it is said that without him, or someone like him, the Renaissance in Italy and Europe would not have spread so rapidly. It was Aldus who put the classics into the hands of the new middle class, which had acquired new wealth and sought the same privileges and cultural opportunities for themselves as possessed by the nobility. Aldus produced well over 1,200 titles, some still in existence.

If you were to ask Aldus he would have told you that publishing the Greek classics was his most important accomplishment. More than 90 percent of his production was devoted to this area. It is said that he made a rule that nothing but Greek should be spoken in his shop during the work day so as to create a more classical atmosphere. Aldus's contributions to the heritage of printing and typography go far beyond the publishing of

THE JENSON FACE (1470)

FIRST ITALIC TYPEFACE CUT BY GRIFFO FOR ALDUS

Bembo ·TB-51
abcdefghijklmnopqrstuvwxyz
ABCDEFGHIJKLMNOPQRSTUVWXYZ
1234567890 (&.,:;!?'""-*$¢%/£)

Bembo Italic ·TB-52
abcdefghijklmnopqrstuvwxyz
ABCDEFGHIJKLMNOPQRSTUVWXYZ
1234567890 (&.,:;!?'""-*$¢%/£)

CURRENT DESIGN BASED ON ALDUS' AND GRIFFO'S BEMBO

ABCDEFGHIJKLMNOPQRSTUV
WXYZ 1234567890
abcdefghijklmnopqrstuvwxyz

ABCDEFGHIJKLMNOPQRSTUV
WXYZ 1234567890
abcdefghijklmnopqrstuvwxyz

NEW DESIGN CREATED BY HERMANN ZAPF AND NAMED FOR
ALDUS

Greek texts. They are both numerous and conspicuous. He was an eminent scholar-printer, one of the first and most influential. Others were more commercially successful, but few have had the lasting impact made by his Dolphin Press. The prestige of the press grew almost spontaneously. It survived attacks in his lifetime, and not only survived, but flourished, in the four and a half centuries since his death.

Aldus's roman type, which inspired the work of Garamond and countless other designers, is a milestone in typographic achievement. Few typeface designs have had such a profound and long-lasting influence on succeeding development efforts. The Aldine italic design, although fashionable to criticize by current standards, became the model for most subsequent italic types. When first shown, it met with great and almost instant success. Although its creation was motivated more by business than altruistic reasons, the final product displaced all previously designed cursives and added an important, valuable tool to typographic communication.

## THE REAL CONTRIBUTION

Aldus holds a firm position as an advocate of education and a catalyst of social improvement. Even though his books were not produced as inexpensive volumes for less fortunate readers, his decision to enter the printing and publishing trade and to give up the secure and comfortable life of a well-patronized scholar, must have arisen out of a goal to bring education and learning to a wider audience. His work meant that eventually students would no longer have to rely on manuscripts and libraries of the wealthy. Because of Aldus's work that dependence became a thing of the past. Education became more accessible to individuals. Before Aldus, students gathered around their "masters" to listen as manuscripts and large, expensive books were read aloud. Aldus's legacy is that of students poring over texts of their own or peopling a library, taking advantage of vast quantities of books and making individual interpretations about what they read.

Aldus died in 1515 at the age of 65. It is said that as he lay in state, his prized possessions—his books—were grouped around him.

# Claude Garamond

### d. 1567

Claude Garamond spent much of his time dissatisfied. Ironic, because today he is considered one of the most respected, influential, and important individuals in typographic history. His skill was such that he received a royal commission from the French court to create a series of typefaces, and his work was in demand by the finest printers of 16th-century France. He was one of the first to establish type founding as an enterprise. Clearly, Garamond was the most important type designer and punch cutter of his time. And yet he wanted more.

Garamond's work brought him into close contact with the most prominent, influential, and wealthiest patrons of the French book arts. This was the source of his dissatisfaction, for he soon became disenchanted with his own small opportunities and profits as a type designer and founder. In the introduction to a book on which he collaborated, he complained that his work "feathers the nest of publishers and brings honey to their hive." Perhaps the mixed metaphors indicate Garamond's mixed feelings about his profession.

## THE DISTINGUISHED PIONEER OF TYPE

Garamond was the most distinguished type designer of his time, perhaps of the entire Renaissance. A true typographic innovator, he was instrumental in the adoption of roman typeface designs in France as a replacement for the commonly used gothic, or blackletter. He was one of the first type designers to create obliqued capitals to complement an italic lowercase and to create an italic design as the companion to a roman type style. Garamond was a pioneer.

Garamond's genius was released because of the influence of another. Geoffroy Tory was Garamond's mentor. Tory was a true Renaissance scholar, a many-sided genius. Originally a teacher of philosophy, he developed an enthusiasm for and love of typography and the graphic arts. This led to energetic experimenta-

tion in engraving, printing, and eventually publishing.

Tory was a native of France but spent several years in Italy. His Italian sojourn profoundly affected Tory's work and philosophy. By the time he returned to France, he had established himself as a bookseller, engraver, and printer. Soon he became the most powerful Italian influence in these crafts. Tory brought warmth, balance, and humanity to the French book arts.

Garamond was one of Tory's most ardent followers. Thus it was that the type Garamond created under Tory's direction followed the roman style of letter then prevalent in Italy. Through Tory's enthusiastic influence and Garamond's remarkable skill as a type designer and punch cutter, roman letterforms began to replace blackletter as the French typographic norm. It has been said that, were it not for the work of Garamond, the French—like the Germans—would have been reading blackletter well into the 20th century.

The genealogy of the current English alphabet is mixed and complicated. The present standard of a root design for capitals, small capitals, lowercase letters, numerals, and corresponding italic and bold designs began in the sixth century but was not given a popular typographic form until the work of Garamond.

## SLANTED LETTERS

The first typefaces were upright designs: the gothics of northern Europe and the romans of Italy. There were no italics. Italic typefaces evolved from the common written hand and were first cast in metal to solve an economic problem. In the Renaissance, knowledge through reading first became accessible to common people, but books were still very elaborate and expensive. Sensing the need and economic opportunity for a reasonably priced product, publishers began to issue books that were more utilitarian in design. Rich ornamentation and grand illustrations were the first embellishments to disappear from these forerunners of the modern "paperback." Next, the size of books was reduced to save paper. As books became smaller, type was designed in smaller sizes. Readability soon began to suffer. In an attempt to return acceptable levels of readability to these inexpensive books, printers began to cast type based on calligraphic letterforms and proportions, because they took less space than traditional romans. The first italics normally consisted of only lowercase characters; when capitals were needed, the printer pulled them from the roman font.

Like many other designers of the period, Garamond also created italic typefaces for this new kind of book. But his italics had complementary sloping capital letters. Although he did not start this trend, his designs were so important that they set the precedent for future work by others. Perhaps even more basic to current standards of typeface design, Garamond's italics were created as harmonious counterparts of roman typefaces. Before Garamond's works, italics and roman typefaces were viewed as two separate typographic tools with distinctively different purposes. Garamond created orderly and elegant typefaces in which all the

parts—capitals, lowercase letters, and italic variants—are balanced contributors to the typographic whole. Because of his creativity and regard for typographic integrity, it is unlikely that Garamond's first italics would have been mere copies.

About this time, Garamond began to resent the financial differences between himself and the publishers for whom he worked. Garamond reasoned that if he published books as an adjunct to his type founding business, he could begin to rectify the differences in monetary rewards. The trouble was that publishing was a very expensive business to enter. Garamond eventually found a business partner, Jean de Gagny, then chancellor of the Sorbonne. De Gagny promised to give financial aid, provided that the type designer would produce "as close a copy as possible of the italic letter Aldus Manutius." (The Aldine italic was the most popular choice for 16th-century French book work.) Garamond agreed, and accordingly, the scheme went forward. Two italics were cut and shown to potential collaborators. The results were deemed favorable, and in 1544, Garamond presented his italic to the French court and was granted a three-year copyright to the design. The following year,

PAGE OF GREC DU ROI: ESTIENNE, PARIS, 1551

ROMAN TYPE (GARAMOND) USED BY ESTIENNE, PARIS, 1549

Garamond (Berthold)
abcdefghijklmnopqrstuvwxyz
ABCDEFGHIJKLMNOPQRSTUVWXYZ

Garamond 156 (Monotype)
abcdefghijklmnopqrstuvwxyz
ABCDEFGHIJKLMNOPQRSTUVWXYZ

Garamond (Stempel)
abcdefghijklmnopqrstuvwxyz
ABCDEFGHIJKLMNOPQRSTUVWXYZ

Garamond 3 (Linotype)
abcdefghijklmnopqrstuvwxyz
ABCDEFGHIJKLMNOPQRSTUVWXYZ

Grafotechna Garamond
abcdefghijklmnopqrstuvwxyz
ABCDEFGHIJKLMNOPQRSTUVWXYZ

Garamont (Amsterdam)
abcdefghijklmnopqrstuvwxyz
ABCDEFGHIJKLMNOPQRSTUVWXYZ

ITC GARAMOND

CURRENT GARAMOND TYPES

his first book was published. In all, five books were jointly published by Garamond and his collaborators. In 1546, however, Garamond gave up his publishing career, having enjoyed little financial success or personal satisfaction.

## GARAMOND STARTS A TRADITION

Garamond is generally credited with establishing the first type foundry. He was the first designer to create faces, cut punches, and then sell the type produced from the punches. Unfortunately, Garamond also had little success in this business. In fact, when he died he owned little more than his punches, and shortly after his death in 1561, his widow was forced to sell even these.

While Garamond was not personally successful, his typefaces certainly were. Eventually they became popular throughout Europe. They found their way to Holland via Christopher Plantin; to Germany through Andre Wechel, the executor of the Garamond estate; and to Italy via Guillaume Le Be, one of Garamond's students. Garamond's work was emulated and copied in nearly all of literary Europe. In France, Garamond's work

became a national style; his punches were used to create and inspire the creation of many type fonts. Some of his punches were even identified as having become part of the original equipment of the French Royal Printing Office, established in Paris by Cardinal Richelieu almost a hundred years after Garamond's death. Richelieu used the type, referred to as the Caracteres de l'Université, in the printing of his book *Les Principaux Poincts de la Foy Catholique Defendus*. It is on this type that most of the modern Garamonds are based.

As with most typestyles, the Garamond designs did not enjoy uninterrupted popularity. After a time, new French designs and styles created by English, Dutch, and Italian foundries, began to replace Garamond's type as the design of choice among printers. It wasn't until the beginning of the twentieth century that new versions of the Garamond style began to appear again in print shops.

One of the first modern Garamonds, Morris Fuller Benton's design for American Type Founders in 1919, met with almost instant success, and other major foundries brought out their versions in quick succession. In 1921, Frederic Goudy completed Garamont, a similar design inspired by the same source, for Lanston Monotype. The English Monotype Company followed in 1924 with its own interpretation of Garamond, again inspired by the Caracteres de l'Université. Once again, the Garamond designs were immensely popular.

In 1926, however, a lengthy and well-documented article by Paul Beaujon, *The Fleuron,* established that Jean Jannon, who worked more than 80 years after Garamond's death, was the first to bring out these first Garamond revivals. Jannon was a printer and punch cutter in Paris. Early in his career, he came into contact with, and was obviously impressed by, the original work of Garamond. In the early 17th century, Jannon's Protestant sympathies took him to Sedan, north of Paris, where he worked in a Calvinist academy.

Because Jannon had difficulty securing tools and materials for his work, he made many of his own. Type was one such tool. Over a period of time, friction between Jannon and the authorities in Sedan resulted in his return to Paris. He took his type and punches with him and worked for only a short time before his Protestant leanings got him into trouble. Jannon was forced to leave Paris, again, but not before his type and punches were confiscated by the government. These eventually found their way into the French National Printing Office, where they were used by Cardinal Richelieu. The type was then placed in the Printing Office archives, where it remained in obscurity for more than two hundred years.

In 1845, the type was rediscovered and pressed into use by the Imprimerie

---

72 Point    4A 6a

# Marks

30 Point    8A 14a

## RESIGNS
## Helps Girl

60 Point    5A 7a

# Sighted

24 Point    9A 19a

## ROMANCE
## Gay songbird
## returns home

48 Point    6A 10a

# Eruption

42 Point    6A 11a

# MODELS
# Delighted

18 Point    15A 29a

MONUMENTS
BEGUN memorial
dedicated to hero

16 Point    17A 34a

ENTERPRISING
FRENCH musicians
banqueted by club

36 Point    7A 12a

# INSPIRED
# Huge Clock

14 Point    22A 42a

BRIGHT PERSONS
NUMBER among your
virtues piety and truth

24 Point    10A 19a

*DIGESTION*
*Fine samples of*
*imported frocks*
*attract maiden*

18 Point    16A 28a

*MISCONSTRUE*
*Conscientious effort*
*stamps the work of*
*true craftsmanship*

16 Point    17A · 34a

*GOVERNMENTS*
*Eastern organization*
*distributing religious*
*tracts through station*

14 Point    22A 44a

*NOBLE PRIVILEGE*
*Pleasingly designed type*
*faces favorably influence*
*the cause of fine printing*

48 Point    6A 10a

# *FORCED*
# *Displayed*

42 Point    7A 12a

# *HOMING*
# *New Basket*

36 Point    7A 12a

# *METHODS*
# *Unfrequented*

30 Point    9A 16a

*ECONOMIZE*
*Color in printing*
*is very attractive*

GARAMOND, AMERICAN TYPE FOUNDERS SPECIMEN BOOK,
1934

GARAMOND, AMERICAN TYPE FOUNDERS SPECIMEN BOOK,
1934

National in Paris, which, two years later, printed two specimen books showing the type and attributing it to Garamond. At the turn of the century, the director of the French National Printing Office studied the material and affirmed that the type was indeed the work of Claude Garamond.

## More Than the Truth about Garamond Is Discovered

Paul Beaujon discovered a specimen book of Jannon's in The Mazarin Library in Paris. After careful and exhaustive research, Paul Beaujon proved that the Garamond types residing in the National Printing Office were actually the work of Jannon, a revelation that caused a sensation in the typographic world. This discovery was perhaps equaled only by the revelation that the man Paul Beaujon was actually a woman, Beatrice Warde, writing under a pseudonym. Printing and typography were "man's business" at the turn of the century and Ms. Warde must have believed that no one would believe the theories of a mere woman. This "mere" woman, however, went on to become a major force at the English Monotype Company and one of the most celebrated historians of the typographic arts. Few people (men or women) have surpassed her accomplishments.

Meanwhile, other Garamond designs were being created. These were based on the type produced by Claude Garamond himself. George Jones of England in 1924 created a design based on an original Garamond. It was released by Linotype & Machinery of London, and

for some unknown reason it was not named Garamond, but Granjon, who was a contemporary of Garamond's. In 1925, both Mergenthaler Linotype and Stempel released designs based on the actual type of Claude Garamond.

## The Style Continues

The *Fleuron* article did little to affect the popularity of the Jannon-based Garamond designs. In fact the styles became so popular that they were duplicated by other foundries: Interetype, in 1927; Mergenthaler Linotype, in 1936; and Monotype, in 1938. To distinguish them from earlier designs, the Linotype version is called Garamond No. 3, and the Monotype is American Garamond.

Over a period of five years, International Typeface Corporation released a large Garamond family of 16 designs. This most recent addition to the Garamond lineage brought the design concept full circle. ITC Garamond was created as a harmonious family of faces in which all the variations are balanced contributors.

Thus, the irony: that the designs of a dissatisfied type designer who died penniless would influence the design of a score of typeface families bearing his name and that the various versions would account for some of the most consistently popular type styles of the last 75 years.

Like most people, Garamond had frailties. Unlike most people, he was exceptionally talented and profoundly creative. He was responsible for popularizing the current standards of harmony in type family development, and for providing the typographic community with one of its most elegant communication tools.

*William Caslon*

1692–1760

Once a month, William Caslon hosted a party at his home. These special evenings were dedicated to good food, hearty ale (usually brewed by Caslon himself), friendly conversation, and beautiful music. Often, the music was provided by eminent masters of the day. Caslon enjoyed those parties and the music that was their unifying theme — almost as much as he enjoyed the financial success that made them possible.

William Caslon designed very beautiful typefaces that changed the course of British typographic history. The father of the Caslon typeface was also a very wealthy man. Shrewd in business, he made money quickly and easily. Also devoted to life's gentler arts, Caslon loved literature, drama, the fine art of conversation, and above all, music. Once his financial success allowed him to do so, Caslon shared these many loves with friends and acquaintances. Throughout his life, Caslon was able to combine business with art, pragmatism with passion. (Perhaps, to some degree, this explains why he married three times.) Many artistic people are also successful in business, but few have been able to combine these seemingly diverse aspects of art and business with the ease and natural grace of William Caslon.

## BEAUTIFUL BRITISH TYPES

Caslon's art was that of typeface design. His types were immediately recognized as exceptionally beautiful communication tools. Typographers and printers throughout Europe unanimously praised his work and made the Caslon designs overnight successes. What makes Caslon's typefaces even more extraordinary is that they were not evolutionary designs based on the firm foundation of earlier work. Prior to Caslon, British type founding and type design standards were at an all-time low. Type founding was a lost art, and new faces that were released were little more than poor copies of designs from other European countries. Caslon's types sprang from barren typographic ground; the quality of his typefaces is more remarkable than if they were produced in a friendly and nurturing environment. Caslon type set the benchmark for all future type design in Britain. Historians have said that, just as Shakespeare gave England a national theater, William Caslon gave the country a national typeface.

Most type critics and historians contend that, given sufficient talent, it is relatively easy to create beautiful typefaces, but that it is altogether more difficult to produce a type of high utilitarian value. Caslon was able to do both. For over 200 years, Caslon was the typeface of choice among printers and typographers. It was used to set nearly every form of printed material: from fine books to high-pressure advertising, to the most mundane ephemera. Nothing was outside Caslon's capabilities. Everyone specified Caslon. It was a favorite of Benjamin Franklin; the American Constitution and Declaration of Independence were both first typeset in Caslon. George Bernard Shaw, the famous Irish playwright, insisted that all his works be set in Caslon. For generations, the motto among printers was "When in doubt, set it in Caslon." The Caslon style still holds the record for the type that has been copied, revived, reissued, and modified more often than any other style.

## CASLON THE BUSINESSMAN

Caslon's typefaces made him famous. However, it was his type founding company that made him wealthy. He built England's first major type founding business. The enterprise became so successful and so influential, that Caslon's types were sold throughout Europe and eventually eclipsed in popularity all other designs from competitive foundries. Caslon's acumen enabled him to build a business that permitted a comfortable lifestyle and relaxed retirement filled with the things he loved: art, literature, a wide circle of friends, and good music.

INTERIOR OF THE CASLON TYPE FOUNDRY, 1750

Like many other famous type founders and designers, William Caslon did not begin his professional career in the typographic arts. Before he produced any type, he was an accomplished and prominent engraver. Caslon specialized in graving and personalizing gun barrels. Early in his career, his work was highly prized by many wealthy patrons. By all accounts, he could have been as successful in this endeavor as he was at creating type.

Engraving gun barrels would normally not seem to be a prerequisite for designing one of the world's most successful typefaces, yet in the 18th century there were many similarities between this craft and that of typeface design. Both demanded patience, artistic ability, skill with engraving tools, and a steady hand. Caslon developed these skills early, and by age 24 he had established his own highly successful engraving business. In addition to this early profession, Caslon

occasionally took on other small assignments that coincidentally aided in his training for type founding. Silver casting taught him the skill of working with small objects cast from molten metal, while the production of bookbinders' stamps gave him additional expertise in carving letters in relief instead of in an engraved form.

## INTRODUCTION TO THE WORLD OF TYPOGRAPHY

It was through these latter two crafts that William Caslon was eventually introduced to the typographic arts. John Watts, a successful bookbinder, and William Bowyer, a noted British printer, became aware of Caslon's artistic ability and engraving skills, and commissioned his services on several occasions. Watts provided Caslon with his first experience in type design by employing the young craftsman to do lettering and punch cutting for a number of his book covers. He also encouraged Caslon to further pursue his letter-cutting ability, promising him personal support and introductions to many leading printers of the day.

At about the same time, Bowyer saw, in a local bookshop, one of the books for which Caslon had produced the cover engraving. He inquired as to who did the work and was introduced to Caslon. The two men quickly became friends, and as a result Bowyer was delighted to take Caslon to a variety of printing offices and, on one occasion, to a prominent London type foundry. Caslon had never seen this part of the type business. After their return from the foundry, Bowyer asked Caslon if he felt that he could manage both the art and business of producing type. Caslon took a night to think the idea over; the next morning he embarked on a career path that was to change the course of typographic history.

William Caslon opened his fledgling type founding business in a small garret with the help of loans from William Bowyer, John Watts, and James Bettenham, son-in-law to Bowyer, and a prominent London printer. At the outset, Caslon's new business succeeded primarily because of the financial and moral support of his three patrons: Watts, Bowyer, and Bettenham. But his products were of remarkable quality, and in a few months the foundry was able to stand on its own and compete with the best companies in the trade. Within a very short time, Caslon's natural abilities in business and his exceptional talents in type founding turned the tiny garret-based venture into a thriving business.

## THE FIRST BIG JOB

Either Bowyer and Watts provided their new investment with an excellent public relations program, or the 18th-century type community had a grapevine that rivaled the current version, because no sooner had Caslon opened his doors for business, than he received his first important commission.

In 1720, the Society for Promoting Christian Knowledge decided to print a version of the New Testament in Arabic for the Eastern Churches. They required a new font of Arabic type for the purpose, and Caslon, despite his lack of experience in producing such work, was selected for the task. Their decision could be considered especially odd because the Society was already in possession of an Arabic font from a long-established British foundry. Perhaps British Arabic types at the time were as poor as British roman types.

This first typographic commission proved to be more fortunate than even Caslon initially realized. After designing the Arabic type, he produced a specimen sheet to encourage additional sales. To identify the source of the sheet, he also cut a few letters in a roman type—just enough to set the words "William Caslon" as a byline. Perhaps to Caslon, the cutting of these letters was a relatively insignificant act, but to those who saw the printed name it became a pivotal event in typographic history.

Upon seeing the byline, one of England's most respected typographic critics encouraged Caslon to develop a complete font based on the few letters in his name. The critic encouraged Caslon's work and provided enthusiastic evaluations of the young designer's ability to influential British printers and typographers—until the foundries with whom he had long-standing business relationships, fearing a loss of business, advised him to be a little more careful about whom he promoted. As a result, he not only became less enthusiastic about Caslon's new type, he even tried to discourage the novice type founder from continuing work on the project.

Confused and frustrated, Caslon turned to his good friend and patron, William Bowyer, for advice. Bowyer, of course, saw the same rare beauty and grace of letter form that impressed the

ABCD
ABCDE
ABCDEFG
ABCDEFGHI
ABCDEFGHIJK
ABCDEFGHIJKL
ABCDEFGHIKLMN

French Cannon.

Quouſque tan-
dem abutere,
Catilina, pati-
*Quouſque tandem*

DOUBLE PICA ROMAN.
Quouſque tandem abutere, Catilina, patientia noſtra? quamdiu
nos etiam furor iſte· tuus eludet?
quem ad finem ſeſe effrenata jac-
ABCDEFGHJIKLMNOP

GREAT PRIMER ROMAN.
Quouſque tandem abutêre, Catilina, patientia noſtra? quamdiu nos etiam furor iſte tuus eludet? quem ad finem ſeſe effrenata jactabit audacia? nihilne te
nocturnum præſidium palatii, nihil urbis vigiliæ, nihil timor populi, nihil con-
ABCDEFGHIJKLMNOPQRS

ENGLISH ROMAN.
Quouſque tandem abutêre, Catilina, patientia
noſtra? quamdiu nos etiam furor iſte tuus eludet?
quem ad finem ſeſe effrenata jactabit audacia?
nihilne te nocturnum præſidium palatii, nihil
urbis vigiliæ, nihil timor populi, nihil conſen-
ſus bonorum omnium, nihil hic munitiſſimus
ABCDEFGHIJKLMNOPQRSTVUW

PICA ROMAN.
Melium, novis rebus ſtudentem, manu ſua occidit.
Fuit, fuit iſta quondam in hac repub. virtus, ut viri
fortes acrioribus ſuppliciis civem pernicioſum, quam
acerbiſſimum hoſtem coërcerent. Habemus enim ſe-
natuſconſultum in te, Catilina, vehemens, & grave:
non deeſt reip. conſilium, neque autoritas hujus or-
dinis: nos, nos, dico aperte, conſules deſumus. De-
ABCDEFGHIJKLMNOPQRSTVUWX

PARTIAL SHOWING OF THE FIRST BROADSIDE SPECIMEN ISSUED BY
WILLIAM CASLON, 1734

type critic. He in turn provided all the encouragement Caslon needed to complete the font.

## CASLON COPIES

The result was Caslon's original roman, and the basis for all succeeding Caslon designs. Over the years, many replicas, recuttings, and attempted improvements of the original Caslon have been produced.

Caslon's types have not maintained their favor continuously, but have passed through several stages of decline and revival. Although popular at the founding of America, they fell into disuse about 1800, and had little or no further exposure for nearly 60 years. Then, in 1858, Laurence Johnson, a prominent Philadelphia type founder, visited the Caslon Type Foundry in London. There he became interested in the revival of the original Caslon types, and although they had not been produced for some time, convinced the directors of the foundry to cast a complete set for him. When he returned to Philadelphia the following year, he made electrotype matrices from these casts and reintroduced the face under the name "Old Style."

The revived face had reasonable popularity—but certainly not of the magnitude of Helvetica—until 1892, when it was used in the new *Vogue* magazine. About this same time, American Type Founders (ATF) was formed out of 23 smaller businesses, one being the Philadelphia foundry that imported the Caslon types many years previously. ATF re-

The Original

# CASLON

OLDSTYLE

Roman *and Italic*

No. 471

*THIS type face is cast also on the AMERICAN POINT LINE. The difference is entirely in the shortening of several of the descenders. Its catalogue name is CASLON NO. 540 and Caslon Italic No. 540. The sizes are from 6 to 120 point in the roman and from 6 to 96 point in the italic*

ATF'S CASLON NO. 471

named the designs Caslon 471, and made them part of its highly successful promotional program.

## WHAT GOES AROUND, COMES AROUND

Once again, the face enjoyed almost immediate popularity. Other designs based on the Caslon style were quickly produced to cash in on the Caslon name. Within the next several years, at least 20 different fonts, all bearing the Caslon name, were released and promoted to American printers and typographers. By the time the company published its fa-

mous 1923 specimen book, American Type Founders alone had more than 12 different typeface families bearing the name Caslon.

In 1916, Lanston Monotype introduced a copy of Caslon No. 471 and called its version No. 337. Ludlow copied the same face and called it Caslon True-Cut. Other versions of Caslon are called New Caslon, Caslon 137, American Caslon, Caslon Ad, Caslon No. 3, ITC Caslon No. 223 (a display face named after the street number of the design studio where it was created) and its text companion ITC Caslon No. 224 (which carries the number 224 only because it follows 223).

## More Designs from the Master

After the release of his first roman, Caslon cut a number of non-Latin and exotic fonts. A font of Coptic was the first to follow the roman. This face was also cut under the direction of Bowyer, whom Caslon repeatedly acknowledged as the master from whom he learned his art.

Shortly after the Coptic, Caslon produced a "blackletter" that received special praise for its faithful following of the traditional Old English character first used by Wynkyn de Worde. He also cut an Armenian, an Etruscan, a Hebrew, and several other foreign language fonts. All were completed before 1734, the year Caslon produced his foundry's first specimen showing. This famous broadside is arranged in four columns and displays a total of 38 fonts. With the exception of three cut by his son, all are Caslon's own handiwork and represent the untiring commitment of 14 years. The exceptional quality and breadth of this work placed Caslon absolutely without rival at the head of his profession in England.

## Can Bad Type Produce a Good Font?

The virtually instantaneous and long-lived success of the Caslon type was not due to coldly flawless perfection like that found in the work of Bodoni or Baskerville. In fact, the Caslon design has been berated by many critics, who have called it crude and inconsistent. But his goal was not to design beautiful letters; it was to create a beautiful type font. Even his most ardent critics agree that talent and mastery of the science of type design had produced letters that are vibrant examples of the typographic art. Text copy, as a mass, appears perfect in spite of the individuality of each letterform. Caslon's types were able to produce that rare circumstance in which the total is something greater than the sum of its parts.

From time to time, Caslon's ability to make money overpowered his talent to create beautiful type. On one such occasion, his desire to increase the size of his inventory almost caused him to not only jeopardize his business, but also to put the future of the Caslon types at risk. In 1728, one of the four main London type foundries was put up for sale. The foundry had been ineffectively managed, sold poor-quality fonts, and was a prime example of the degraded state of the British typographic industry. Caslon thought that he could purchase the business at much less than the asking price and made a ridiculously low bid, much lower than the seller was willing to accept.

The good news (although certainly Caslon did not think so at the time) was that the deal fell through. Had Caslon been burdened by a large and essentially useless stock of matrices, they would almost inevitably have been mingled with his own beautiful work. The end result might have been a patchwork of dissimilar types in which the bad greatly outnumbered the good.

Caslon had these flashes of acquisition fever on other occasions, and many times the results yielded larger inventory. Fortunately, his purchases were considerably smaller and of better quality than the deal that could have ruined his business and the Caslon type heritage.

## How It All Began

William Caslon was born in the West Midland village of Cradley. His birth, in 1692, was recorded in the parish register as "child of George Casselon by Mary his wife." Tradition has it that the surname was originally Caslona, after an Andalusian town from which William Caslon's father migrated to England.

Villagers in 17th-century England were often brought into the trade of the area. Children learned their craft under apprenticeship contracts arranged by their parents. The process usually entailed a strictly disciplined, seven-year learning program, in which an apprentice served first as an indentured servant, then as a journeyman until the young worker was invited to join the craft's guild.

William Caslon began his career under very similar circumstances. While his father was a shoemaker by trade, the area where Caslon was born was part of a growing weapons industry. Most of the metal gun parts were produced in Midland forges and then sent to London, where they were assembled and joined to wooden stocks. It was also in London where the engraving and trademark initials were crafted.

Caslon's artistic talent probably displayed itself early, because at age 13 he was indentured not to a tradesman in his own town, but to Edward Cookes, a successful engraver living in London. The story is told that this somewhat unusual arrangement was made because the headmaster at Caslon's school saw raw talent in the boy and helped to set up the indenture program with Cookes, his daughter's husband.

Caslon was declared a "free man of London" in 1717 but continued to work for Cookes until he established his own business a year later. Even after Caslon left the employment of his teacher, Cookes and his family continued to have a profound influence on Caslon's early career. His first wife, Sarah Pearman, was Cookes' niece; and the first employee of Caslon's own firm was a nephew of Cookes.

## LEARNING THE "SECRET" CRAFT

Caslon worked as an engraver for several years, building a successful business, before he learned the craft of type founding, still a closely guarded secret in 18th-century England. To produce type was to be involved in the spread of printing and bookselling, trades dominated by government censorship and imposed monopolies. Only 50 or 60 years earlier, all British publishing was completely controlled by church and state. It was William Bowyer who provided Caslon with the opportunity to enter the profession that made him artistically renowned and financially successful.

Caslon carried on business out of his first small foundry until 1727, when he moved to larger quarters on Iron Monger Row. By 1730 his fame was such that many of the most important British printing houses were using his type. He even secured rights for the exclusive use of his fonts by the King's Printers.

In 1737 Caslon's growing business forced him to move once again to a larger space, this time to the now-famous Chiswell Street Foundry. It was here that his son and succeeding generations of Caslons, carried on the family business for more than 120 years.

By 1742, Caslon had printed his second specimen sheet. This one showed 12 fonts created by his son, William Caslon II, who had just been made a partner in the business. Young Caslon proved to be as able as his father and soon managed enough of the firm's day-to-day business to allow the senior Caslon to participate in more administrative activities.

At 57, Caslon was appointed Justice of the Peace for Middlesex by King George II. This was a tribute to his stature and importance to the British government and prominence within his community. Having lived to see the results of his ability as an artist and businessman, Caslon retired, universally respected, from active management of his company, free and financially able to pursue more artistic enjoyments.

On January 23, 1766, at the age of 74, William Caslon died at his country house in Bethnal Green.

Like the music of many of the musicians who performed in Caslon's house, his work lives on. To be able to create beautiful works of art is one thing. To have these pieces of art be considered highly utilitarian tools is something else. And to have these beautiful, utilitarian tools used consistently for more than 200 years is, indeed, something quite remarkable. William Caslon made truly remarkable type.

# John Baskerville

## 1706–1775

John Baskerville was cranky and vain and scornful of convention. He has been called a dilettante, an eccentric, and unattractive. His peers disapproved of him, his type, and his printing. Clearly, Baskerville was not popular.

Baskerville broke the rules of his craft to create what he believed was perfect printing and, in doing so, he alienated almost all of his contemporaries. While not enhancing his popularity rating, his breaking with the accepted traditions of printing changed the course of typographic development.

The trouble began with his type design. The face he created was light and delicate, much more so than previous styles. It had contrasts in stroke weights that were more pronounced than those of any other face. Baskerville's type could not be reproduced properly with accepted printing technology, so he began to improve the technology. He refined the design of the printing press, had paper developed specially for his needs, and invented the hot-pressing process. His method of printing was so closely connected with the design and effect of his type that the two should not be considered separately.

John Baskerville was never to know the profound impression he made on the printing craft. Printers and typophiles of the day poked fun at his smooth paper and claimed that his light type was unreadable.

Benjamin Franklin was one of the few on Baskerville's side. He met the Birmingham printer during one of his trips to England. Franklin purchased several of Baskerville's books and fonts of his type and frequently championed his cause among American printers who felt that Baskerville's type was unfit for reading. Franklin and Baskerville corresponded often, and in one letter Franklin related a trick he played on an American friend. Upon hearing the friend complain that Baskerville's type could be "the means of blinding all the readers in the Nation owing to the thin and narrow strokes of the letters," Franklin decided to test the validity of the complaint.

Probably with a twinkle in his eye, he gave a friend a specimen sheet of Caslon, calling it Baskerville's, and asked for specific criticism. Franklin wrote that his friend eagerly undertook the challenge and "went over several Fonts, showing me everywhere he thought Instances of that Disproportion" and declared, before he finished, that his eyes were suffering from "Baskerville Pains."

Undaunted, Baskerville persisted in the development and use of his type. In fact, in the design, production, and use of his type, he set an example of thoroughness that few have equaled. He worked for more than six years on the design, drawing and redrawing the basic shapes thousands of times. Only when he was completely satisfied did he establish his own type foundry and employ a punch cutter. In the process, Baskerville became the first type designer.

It would be two years before his first types were cut, and several more before the first book using them was printed. One reason Baskerville was able to be so thorough, to take such pains in developing and using his faces, was that he was an amateur; this work was for pleasure. He did not accumulate his sizable fortune from the sale of his books and type. Those items usually found their way into the "red column" of his ledger sheet.

Baskerville's livelihood derived from the production of japanned goods, one of Birmingham's chief industries. Japanning is the decoration of metal articles (candleholders, tea trays, bread baskets, etc.) with multiple coats of varnish. The articles are then further decorated with paintings of fruits, flowers, and pastoral scenes. Baskerville had many rivals in the japanning trade and must have had to concentrate much of his time and commercial acumen to keep ahead of them. The intensive effort in japanning forced Baskerville to move slowly in his typographic endeavors and to work out of love rather than from monetary motivation. It has been suggested that the japanning trade also gave Baskerville the idea for hot pressing, a process he felt was vital

*Double Pica Roman.*

TANDEM aliquando, Quirites! L. Catilinam furentem audacia, ſcelus anhelantem, pe-
ABCDEFGHIJKLMN.

*Great Primer Roman.*

TANDEM aliquando, Quirites! L. Catilinam furentem audacia, ſcelus anhelantem, peſtem patriæ nefarie molientem, vobis atque huic urbi ferrum flam-
ABCDEFGHIJKLMNOP.

Double Pica Italic.

*TANDEM aliquando, Quirites! L. Catilinam furentem audacia, ſcelus anhelantem, peſtem patriæ nefarie moli-*
*ABCDEFGHIJKLMN.*

Great Primer Italic.

*TANDEM aliquando, Quirites! L. Catilinam furentem audacia, ſcelus anhelantem, peſtem patriæ nefarie molientem, vobis atque huic urbi ferrum flammamque minitan-*
*ABCDEFGHIJKLMNOPQR.*

TYPES FROM BASKERVILLE'S BORDERED
BROADSIDE SPECIMEN, 1762

THE

Holy Bible,

CONTAINING THE

OLD TESTAMENT

AND

*THE NEW:*

Tranſlated out of the

Original Tongues,

AND

With the former TRANSLATIONS

Diligently Compared and Reviſed,

*By His MAJESTY's Special Command.*

APPOINTED TO BE READ IN CHURCHES.

*CAMBRIDGE,*

Printed by *JOHN BASKERVILLE,* Printer to the UNIVERSITY.
MDCCLXIII.

*CUM PRIVILEGIO.*

TITLE PAGE OF THE 1763 BIBLE

to the proper printing from his types. When paper is made by hand, as it was in Baskerville's time, it has a rough, uneven surface. Handmade paper is also so strong and resistant that it must be dampened before printing, which tends to roughen the surface even more. None of this was compatible with the printing of Baskerville's delicate types, so he hit on the idea of pressing the wet sheets between hot copper plates after they left the press. This smoothed the paper considerably and also helped to set the ink.

Baskerville had a ready supply of copper plates available as part of the goods used to manufacture the japanned articles. He was also familiar with the process of heating and baking the metal in the decorating process.

We would find little difference between Baskerville's hot-pressed paper and the bound paper commonly used today. His contemporaries, however, found little room for comparison with even their finest papers. It was referred to as being "so glossy and of such perfect polish that one would suppose the paper made of silk rather than linen."

Baskerville's critics argued that his paper was so shiny that it compounded the problem of dazzling caused by his typeface designs.

Ink was the only product of Baskerville's typographic efforts that escaped criticism. His ink was the envy of his peers. One printer described it, almost lovingly, as "partaking of a peculiarly soft luster, bordering upon a deep purple."

In the 18th century, printers didn't buy ink; they made their own. Many of the recipes were closely guarded secrets. Baskerville's was such a secret. It was claimed, for instance, that one of his tricks was to age the ink for three years before putting it to use. But whatever the total process was, it worked. Even today, few inks are as dark and as rich as Baskerville's.

Making the ink was just the first step in the printing process. Next, it had to be transferred from the type to the paper—no easy task in the middle 1700s. Few improvements to the printing press had been made since Gutenberg's day. The press was still essentially two flat surfaces forced together by a hand screw, and it was certainly too inaccurate and unreliable to faithfully reproduce Baskerville's type. As he did with ink, Baskerville made his own printing press, a state-of-the-art machine in 18th-century England.

Baskerville himself, with characteristic lack of modesty, describes it as "exactly on the same Construction of other Peoples but perhaps more accurate than any ever formed since the Invention of the Art of Printing. . . ."

Finally, there was paper. Again, the standard product of the day was not suited to the faithful printing of Baskerville's type. As a result, he spent many hours experimenting with paper and paper making. He even had a small paper mill built on his property. Because of those extensive experiments, and because he was the first to use what is now called "wove" paper in books, Baskerville is often credited with its invention.

Wove paper is formed on a closely woven thin-wire mesh that leaves the finished sheet quite smooth. In contrast, laid paper (the common paper of the 18th century) is textured because the fibers lie on a crude wire mesh as the sheets form.

While Baskerville's name is almost always associated with the introduction of wove paper, and he certainly had a hand in its development, records of the paper merchant he dealt with indicate that the invention was the combined work of several hands. Thus it was Baskerville who first made ink, printing technology, and paper conform to the needs of typeface design, instead of vice versa. This feat has rarely been matched. It is especially sad that, despite all his time, labor, and expense, Baskerville's types did not meet with much approval.

This, however, may have been as much for moral as for esthetic reasons. Eighteenth-century Britons had particular disdain for deviants from two accepted moral standards: agnostics and adulterers. Baskerville was both.

It did not matter that the woman Baskerville lived with had been deserted by her husband. She was married, but not to the Birmingham type founder. Baskerville did marry Sarah Eaves shortly after her husband died, but the sixteen years of adulterous living could not go unnoticed nor uncensured in 18th-century British society.

The other flawed aspect of John Baskerville's character was his opposition to Christianity, an aversion that was lifelong and consistent. Typical of his feelings are those represented in his will: "I have a hearty contempt for all superstition, the farce of a consecrated ground, the Irish barbarism of sure and certain hopes, etc. I also consider revelation as it is called, exclusive of the scraps of morality casually intermixed with it, to be the most impudent abuse of common sense whichever was invented to befool mankind." For several more sentences the will continues to expound on the "ignorant and bigoted, who . . . profess to believe as they call it certain absurd doctrines and mysteries. . . ."

John Baskerville was the last child of John and Sahra Baskerville. (It is interesting to note that John was his father's namesake, and his wife shared his mother's name.) He was born in late 1704 or early in 1705, in Worcestershire, England.

PUBLII VIRGILII

MARONIS

BUCOLICA,

GEORGICA,

ET

AENEIS.

BIRMINGHAMIAE:

Typis JOHANNIS BASKERVILLE.

MDCCLVII.

TITLE PAGE OF BASKERVILLE'S *AENEID* BY VIRGIL

# PREFACE.

AMONGST the feveral mechanic Arts that have engaged my attention, there is no one which I have purfued with fo much fteadinefs and pleafure, as that of *Letter-Founding*. Having been an early admirer of the beauty of Letters, I became infenfibly defirous of contributing to the perfection of them. I formed to my felf Ideas of greater accuracy than had yet appeared, and have endeavoured to produce a *Sett* of *Types* according to what I conceived to be their true proportion.

*Mr. Caflon* is an Artift, to whom the Republic of Learning has great obligations; his ingenuity has left a fairer copy for my emulation, than any other mafter. In his great variety of *Characters* I intend not to follow him; the *Roman* and *Italic* are all I have hitherto attempted; if in thefe he has left room for improvement, it is probably more owing to that variety which divided his attention, than to any other caufe. I honor his merit, and only wifh to derive fome fmall fhare of Reputation, from an Art which proves accidentally to have been the object of our mutual purfuit.

After having fpent many years, and not a

A 3                                          little

PAGE OF BASKERVILLE'S PREFACE TO MILTON'S, BIRMINGHAM, 1758

His family was upper-middle class.

He received his first professional recognition at 17, when his remarkable calligraphic skill was noticed and he was given the duties of writing master in the parish school. During this time he also began to cut gravestones. There are no known examples of his work extant, but there is a slate slab preserved in the Birmingham Reference Library that was intended as an advertisement for his services.

When Baskerville was approximately 34, his father died, leaving him a substantial sum of money. It was also about this time that he entered the japanning trade, which provided him with a handsome living for the rest of his life.

Baskerville was well past 40 when his interest in typography began. The first example of his work (the Latin *Virgil*) was published in 1757. In 1758, he followed with a two-volume edition of Milton. In the preface he wrote, "Amongst the several mechanical Arts that engaged my attention, there is no one which I have pursued with so much steadiness and pleasure, as that of Letter-Founding. Having been an early admirer of the beauty of Letters, I became insensibly desirous of contributing to the perfection of them. I formed to my self Ideals of greater accuracy than had yet appeared, and have endeavored to produce a Sett of Types according to what I conceived to be their true proportion."

By 1758, Baskerville had produced eight fonts of type. It was then that he offered his designs for sale and received the rebuff that later caused him to repent the day he entered the printing and type founding business. Nevertheless, he continued to practice his craft until his death at age 69. He was buried in a mausoleum he had erected on his own grounds.

The story, however, is not complete. Several years after his death, Baskerville's estate was sold and eventually converted to canal wharves. Sometime during this period, the mausoleum was demolished. Baskerville's remains, however, lay undisturbed, or undetected, until 1820, when workers discovered the grave while digging for gravel. At this time the coffin was moved to a warehouse, where it was opened, the contents viewed, and then resealed. The coffin remained in the warehouse for eight years. It was then moved to the shop of a plumber, where it was again opened, and a local artist made a pencil sketch of the body. It is said that a number of those present at the opening became severely ill, and one Dr. Male died after putting a torn piece of the death shroud in his pocket.

The casket was reinterred in the Church of England cemetery, in a vault below the chapel. This was in February 1898. Finally, Baskerville was laid to a peaceful rest.

As with Baskerville the man, his type was also a long time in achieving a peaceful rest. After his death, his wife turned over much of Baskerville's type to Robert Martin, his senior workman. Four years later, Mrs. Baskerville sold the type and foundry equipment to a publisher for the purpose of printing the works of Voltaire. Fifteen years after his death, Baskerville's type, punches, and matrices were moved to Paris, where they were used for printing during the revolutionary period. Gradually the type fell into disuse and was passed from one French printer to another until the French foundry of Deberny and Peignot purchased the punches and matrices in 1936. Finally in 1953, Deberny and Peignot presented all the punches to the Cambridge University Press.

Baskerville's typefaces were the catalyst for more than a new style of typeface design; they changed the course of typographic development. If he had merely imitated, or even improved upon, the work of his contemporaries, there would be little to say about him today. John Baskerville, however, abandoned tradition and began a movement that was to revolutionize printing and typography of the 18th century. Although his faces were not used—indeed, they were not even liked—his typographic arrangements and design style became a primary influence on the work of Bodoni and Didot. Baskerville's typefaces stand almost alone as a representation of the "transitional style" of typeface design, bridging the gap between the "Oldstyles" of designers like Caslon, and the "Moderns" of Bodoni and Didot.

Baskerville's "unattractive and painful" typeface is today one of the most popular and most-used serif typestyles. It is represented in virtually every type library and can be reproduced on practically any form of type imaging device. Baskerville has become a staple of text typographic communication.

Perhaps Baskerville's scorn for convention was not, in itself, admirable. But the positive and innovative steps he took to replace typographic convention certainly were. Many sources refer to Baskerville as tenacious. He was that, and more. Baskerville was a positive thinker and doer. He replaced the wrong, inaccurate, and imperfect with definite and justified improvements. In addition to his beautiful and now popular typeface, we should remember John Baskerville for his spirit and positive drive.

# Giambattista Bodoni

## 1740–1813

In harmony with his "aristocratic" typefaces, Giambattista Bodoni lived a virtually aristocratic lifestyle. History has given him the title "the king of typographers and the typographer of kings." After a relatively short apprenticeship, Bodoni became almost immediately the director of the royalty press belonging to the Duke of Parma. And a few years later, when Napoleon drove the Austrian governors out of northern Italy, he continued his work under Imperial patronage.

Bodoni created typefaces and typography to impress the eye. His designs were studied efforts meant to be seen as well as read. Few would deny that Bodoni's typefaces are beautiful; unfortunately, few would say they are also easy to read. By current standards, his designs are, in fact, the antithesis of what an easily readable typeface should be. Had he known this fact, however, Bodoni would probably not have been very upset. His goal was not to create type or typography to be appreciated by the masses. His books and other printing exercises were large, regal efforts meant to be looked upon and appreciated as works of art, rather than as mere pieces of communication. His work was probably the most honored—and least read—printing of his time.

The typography Bodoni produced is still regarded as being among the most refined and structured printing ever produced. But then, he had the luxury of virtually limitless time, money, and effort to spend on any given project. Bodoni once confided to a friend that he agonized more than six months and produced thousands of trial proofs in the process of choosing just the right type for the title page of one of his books!

Luxury of choice and time in Bodoni's craft was complemented by the luxurious lifestyle he was able to maintain. While he did not reside in a palace or command a variety of servants, neither did he have to be concerned where his lira were coming from; Bodoni was paid whether he worked or not. Some historians would have us believe that Bodoni struggled to get by on a meager salary

with inadequate equipment. It's true that his career began in this manner, but by the time he was 40 Bodoni had at least two sources of income. One was a grant from the Duke of Parma, the other was from the printing and publishing he did on his own. By his own account, he was a wealthy man.

While all this grandeur and prosperity certainly must have been gratifying to Bodoni, some suggest that the concept and function of a "royalty press" run counter to the basic premise of typographic communication. Typography, they argue, has a history of providing inexpensive, attractive information to the masses; and, in fact, the first typography in the Western world, Gutenberg's Bible, started this tradition. Daniel Berkeley Updike, in his definitive 19th-century book *Printing Types,* accused Bodoni of caring nothing about printing as a means to instruct or edify the masses. He wrote: "Bodoni did not despise the masses—he forgot all about them! He was a court printer, existing by the patronage of the lucky few. His editions were intended to be *livres d'apparat.* He alone saw no harm in making them so, but the bigger and more pretentious they were, the better he liked them."

## BODONI'S "NEW" TYPE AND TYPOGRAPHY

Bodoni was no revolutionary. The modern roman style, which is attributed to him, did not, as many would believe, spring forth as if by magic. While the letters he cut and the books he printed were more refined and of exceptionally higher quality than most of the work originating before or during his lifetime, it would be difficult to classify any of Bodoni's efforts as fundamentally new. When he was young, the work of John Baskerville served as his ideal; when he opened his first printing office for the Duke of Parma, Bodoni did so with type from Fournier. In later years, the work of his great Parisian competitor, François Didot, influenced him dramatically. Bo-

# IN FVNERE
# CAROLI III
## HISPAN. REGIS CATHOLICI
### *ORATIO*

HABITA

IN SACELLO PONTIFICIO

## A BERNARDINO RIDOLFI

SANCTISS. D. N. PII SEXTI INTIMO CVBICVLARIO

CANONICO VATICANO,

IVDICE ET AVDITORE GENERALI

SAC. CONGR. REV. FABRICAE S. PETRI DE VRBE

### *PARMAE*

EX REGIO TYPOGRAPHEO

M. DCC. LXXXIX

TYPICAL BODONI TREATMENT OF A TITLE PAGE

doni was always, in some manner, dependent on the work of other, bolder contemporaries.

Yet despite these influences, he was not a copyist. A comparison of Bodoni's type to Didot's, two designs that on the surface may appear virtually identical, is a perfect example. There are distinct similarities in their work, and Bodoni surely studied Didot's designs very carefully, but a close examination reveals that Bodoni's weight transitions are more gradual and his serifs still maintain a slight degree of bracketing. There is even a hint of "old style" in Bodoni's work. He followed Didot's lead, carefully evaluating the designs of his great competitor, consciously remaining, however, always just slightly behind the radical modernism of his contemporary. Perhaps

this explains, to some degree, the longevity of Bodoni's type designs. They were radical enough to be considered new and different (to establish for Bodoni an important and influential place in current typographic circles), but not so different that they became the 18th-century versions of fad designs.

## EVOLUTION OF "MODERN" TYPE STYLES

The art of the punch cutter is by nature, conservative, and the history of Roman typeface design bears this out. Once letterforms had their basic shape and proportions determined in the 15th century, noticeable changes were few and far between. In the course of the 18th century,

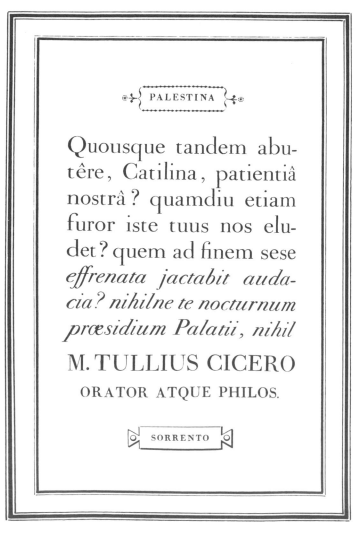

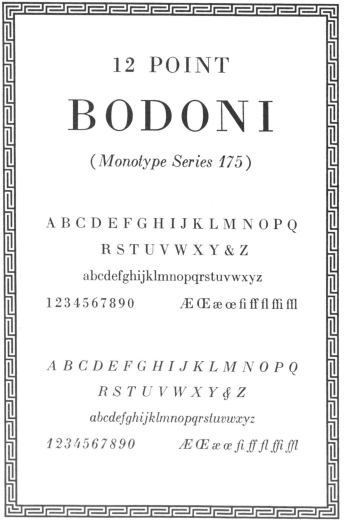

FROM BODONI'S *MANUALE TIPOGRAFICO*

MONOTYPE BODONI

Quuousque tandem abutere, Catili

30 POINT LINOTYPE BODONI

Quuousque tandem abutere, Catili Q

30 POINT MONOTYPE BODONI

Quuousque tandem abutere, Catil

30 POINT INTERTYPE BODONI

Quuousque tandem abutere, Cat

30 POINT ATF BODONI

Quuousque tandem abutere, C

30 POINT BAUER BODONI

CURRENT BODONI TYPES

however, and seemingly without warning, a new and revolutionary style of roman letter made its appearance. It was distinguished from previous "old style" designs by fine hairline serifs, a distinct contrast of thick and thin strokes, and a weight stress that was vertical rather than oblique. This new style of roman letter was the result, not of the warmth and vitality of the calligrapher's brush, but of a logical and mathematical approach to letter form construction.

One of the first of these "logical" typefaces was cut by Phillipe Grandjean under the influence of the engravings of a supposedly "perfect letter" developed by a committee entrusted to the design process by the Paris Academie. Like so many other "designs by committee" neither these letters nor the resulting type from Grandjean proved to have any lasting success. Their worth was in influencing later designers to develop non-calligraphic letterforms.

The work of Pierre Simon Fournier and John Baskerville followed that of Grandjean and echoed the basic design traits and character proportions he established. While Fournier created his type

more than 40 years later than Grandjean, and Baskerville still a decade later, these can be traced as the distinct evolutionary steps toward the moderns of Didot and Bodoni.

## Do Good Moderns Equal Bad Type?

Moderns hold a unique place in typographic history and usage. They mark a departure from previous designs that can only be compared to Jenson's departure from the frakturs of northern Europe, and they are as difficult to use well as any text typeface ever created.

Beatrice Warde, the eminent typographic historian, in a famous essay, likened the perfect type to a crystal goblet. Her perfect type is transparent, or invisible, to the reader and allows the content to be enjoyed without coloration or distraction. Bodoni's type is anything but a "crystal goblet." Its hairline serifs, strong thick-and-thin stroke contrast, and abrupt weight changes cloud the reading process. Bodoni is no quiet servant to the

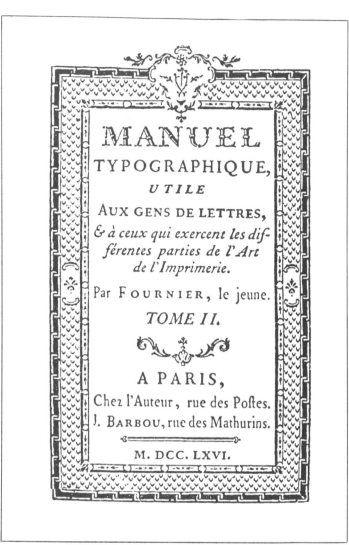

COMPARISON OF FOURNIER'S (A) AND BODONI'S (B) HANDLING OF TITLE PAGES

communication process; it is a design that demands attention.

If used carefully, Bodoni type can create typography that is exceptionally beautiful, even elegant, but not particularly easy to read. If used poorly, Bodoni's extreme weight contrasts and vertical stress can cause a typographic effect, "dazzling," which is visually uninviting and exceptionally disruptive to the reading process. Bodoni makes a very powerful typographic statement—one way or another.

## BODONI'S EARLY YEARS

Giambattista (John the Baptist) Bodoni was born in 1740, in Saluzzo, a relatively small town in northern Italy. He was the fourth and youngest son of Francesco Agostino Bodoni, a master printer in Saluzzo. Three of his four sons also became printers. Domenico succceeded to his father's printing house; Giuseppe assisted his famous brother in Parma; and Giambattista, became one of the most successful and influential printers of all time.

As a boy, Bodoni worked in his father's business, first as a "printer's devil" doing odd, and not particularly pleasant, jobs around the print shop. Later he became a full-fledged apprentice, learning the basic skills of printing and block engraving.

At the age of 18, Bodoni came to the conclusion many young men had reached before, and have since: that it was time to seek growth and learning outside home and away from parents. He and a schoolmate went to Rome. Immediately, Bodoni's talents and the basic education from his father began to pay off. (It is said that much of the cost of the journey was paid by the sale of his engraving blocks to printers in cities and towns along the route.) Once in Rome, Bodoni secured employment in the printing house of the Vatican, a great honor in itself.

Bodoni developed his typographic skills and made important friends in Rome. While working as a compositor at the Vatican press, Bodoni showed an interest in, and eventually took up the study of, oriental languages. He was remarkably successful at these studies. So successful was he that he was given the task of putting in useful order the series of exotic characters that had been cut by the French type designers Garamond and LeBe. These had, through years of misuse, become hopelessly pied (scrambled), and thus useless. This tedious, frustrating, and complicated work brought Bodoni into conferences with many learned officials of the Press, including Cardinal Spinnelli, head of the institution, and Abbot Ruggieri, the superintendent. The abbot was to become a close friend and advisor to the young printer. Through Cardinal Spinnelli, Bodoni also met Father Maria Paciaudi, who was at that time librarian to the Cardinal.

FROM BODONI'S *MANUALE TIPOGRAFICO*

# II
# MODERN PIONEERS

*Frederic W. Goudy*

1865–1947

GOUDY AT AGE EIGHT

FRED AND A CLOSE FRIEND

For some, success comes easily. For others it is a long and difficult process. Frederic Goudy's success falls into the latter category. At a time when most people are firmly established in their careers, Goudy was "just getting by." In fact, there were many times when he and his wife, Bertha, were not even "getting by."

The story was told that once, after working all day and early into the evening at the Village Press, the Goudys were treated to a late dinner by a customer who purchased a $15 book. The prospect of the food that the money would buy was so welcome that the Goudys ran down the 12 flights of stairs from their offices—and reached the street ahead of the customer who had waited for the elevator!

*Undaunted* is perhaps the best single word to describe Fred Goudy. He came to his position of eminence in the typographic world only after years of being dogged by misfortune and lack of success. His career was marked by unprofitable work as a bookkeeper, cashier, private secretary, and copywriter. Goudy had unrewarded spells as a freelance graphic designer, printer, teacher, and typographer. He started two magazines, both of which failed, and various printing businesses, which also failed. It wasn't until Goudy was past the halfway point in his life that he got his first big break and began to receive the recognition he deserved.

## TRAGIC LOSSES

Twice, virtually everything Goudy produced—his precious matrices, his master drawings, and preliminary sketches—were all destroyed by fires. The first was in the early part of 1908.

The Goudys had finally begun to sell some work from the Village Press, and it looked as though they were about to turn the corner of success. They had reached a point where work long into the evening was no longer necessary to make ends meet. On January 10, the Goudys were spending the evening at home. Bertha was sewing and Fred was reading. At

8:30 the telephone rang; Bertha answered. After a conversation that lasted only seconds, she calmly reported, "The Parker Building is on fire, you'd better hurry down."

Goudy dressed rapidly and took the downtown subway from near their apartment to the building that housed the Village Press. He emerged from an exit within the firelines, and the police were forced to usher him to safety. The "fireproof" Parker Building was a veritable furnace. Its brick walls effectively trapped the white-hot interior. Goudy stood on the corner and watched the Village Press disappear. All the books, the equipment, his drawings and sketches were gone.

In 1939, fire once again devastated the Goudys' life work. It was on a frosty morning, again in January, that their mill (the focal point of the Deepdene Press), which contained their machinery, the press, Goudy's matrices and many priceless drawings, burned. Everything settled into the mill stream—leaving intact, ironically, only an unused brick vault that had been built to protect many of the things that were destroyed. Once again, Goudy was forced to stand by and watch fire ruthlessly destroy the products of his labors.

Goudy was undaunted. It was characteristic of him to turn the adversities life imposed upon him into a benefit: His design ability and love of the book arts were developed as a result of the early business failures in his more pedestrian endeavors. Goudy turned to type design and type founding when the 1908 fire deprived him of his printing plant. The final, and more disastrous, fire that destroyed the workshop where he labored for many years, enabled Goudy to devote more of his time to writing and teaching.

## THE LATE BLOOMER

It wasn't until he was 43 that Goudy's type designs began to show the mark of his genius. His earlier typefaces such as Camelot, Pabst, and Powell were good designs, but none achieved the popularity

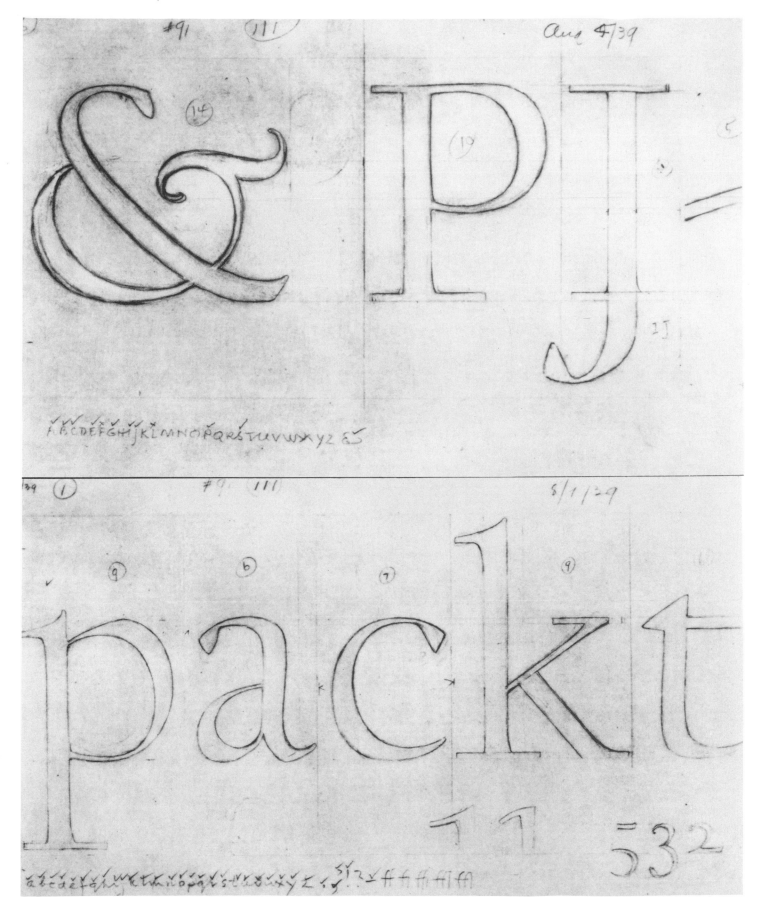

PRELIMINARY SKETCHES OF ONE OF GOUDY'S TYPEFACES

of his later work. His first work after the 1908 fire was the No. 38E series for the Lanston Monotype Machine Company. It was the first design that began to reflect Goudy's capability as a type designer.

In 1910, an incident occurred that brought Goudy international recognition almost overnight. Late in the winter of that year he was asked by Mitchell Kennerley, the publisher, to design a volume of short stories by H. G. Wells. Goudy made layouts for the pages and had dummy copies set in 18-point Caslon. When he received the dummy pages, Goudy was disappointed. They just didn't look quite the way he wanted. There was a feeling of "openness" that disturbed him. Goudy explained to Kennerley that he wanted "the appearance of solidity and compactness, but of the same color as Caslon." Neither he nor Kennerley knew of such a type. Existing typefaces were either too "formal or too refined, or too free and undignified" for use in a book of the kind Goudy was designing.

No other solution to the problem being at hand, Goudy suggested to Kennerley that he create a new face that would meet his requirements. Kennerley agreed, and the work was begun immediately on Kennerley Old Style.

It took only a week to draw the complete alphabet: lowercase, capitals, and punctuation. The italic was completed shortly after, and a complete font of 16-point type had been cut and cast by late March of the following year. It had taken less than five months from start to finish.

When Kennerley Old Style was offered to printers, it was met with such enthusiasm that Goudy soon became the premier American type designer. The release of this type style marked the turning point in Goudy's career. It was the start of a growing fame for the man whose wife-to-be had been warned that he would "never amount to anything."

## A SELF-TRAINED GENIUS

Goudy's achievements are even more remarkable in that he was self-taught, making his first designs at the age of 30, and manufacturing his own type after 60.

The work method Goudy developed was designed for speed. He ruled off the page to be filled and sketched characters swiftly with a pencil. Then with a pen he began the final version, modifying the pencil sketch when necessary as he went along. Only the letter forms were penned in at first. When a line of letters was finished, the sheet was turned on its side and the serifs were drawn in quickly along the ruled lines. Some say this speed of execution gave his letters vigor, life, and movement that would have been lacking with a more studied technique.

Unfortunately, later in Goudy's career, not all printers were equally impressed with the vigor and life in his work. With the advent of the post–World War II "modern" style of typography, typefaces from Europe seemed more attractive than the work of American designers. Some considered Goudy's work old-fashioned. But fortunately for the design community, those "old-fashioned" Goudy designs are now described as "classic" and are used more today than at any previous time.

Frederic W. Goudy was born in Bloomington, Illinois, on March 8, 1865, into a family of Scottish origin. His father was at one time a teacher, a real estate broker, and a judge of the probate court.

The Goudys moved about a good deal. Between 1865 and 1876, his family lived "in four different towns, and in one of them twice." By 1884, the family had located in the Dakota territory. It was here that young Frederic did most of his growing up.

And it was from there, at the age of 23, that he set out on his own career of change and caprice.

## Goudy Oldstyle

**72 Point**  4 A  6 a

# RICH
# Spirits

**60 Point**  5 A  7 a

# MODE
# Highest

**48 Point**  5 A  9 a

# NOTICE
# Bright lad
# leads class

**42 Point**  5 A  10 a

# DANCED
# Celebrated
# big holiday

**36 Point**  6 A  10 a

# HOME
# Quaint

**30 Point**  7 A  14 a

# FOUND
# Musician
# delighted

**24 Point**  8 A  16 a

# NOTICES
# Unfinished
# framework

**18 Point**  12 A  23 a

MECHANIC
Gives experts
usual warning

**14 Point**  17 A  34 a

EXPERIMENTS
BRIGHT magician
spent much time
unraveling tricks

**12 Point**  21 A  40 a

GRAND PICTURE
RECENT photographs
inspire many leading
theatrical promoters

**10 Point**  24 A  48 a

PERFECT SPECIMEN
SIMPLE design exhibited
considered very artistic
for modern typography

**8 Point**  27 A  54 a

CUT-COST EQUIPMENT
MODERN cabinets containing
leads and quads reduce labor
costs considerably. Efficiency
material creates large profits

**6 Point**  29 A  58 a

STIMULATING PRODUCTION
PROGRESSIVE printers recognize the
fact that economy lies in equipping
their plants with modern materials
and machinery. Now is the time, as
every minute lost swells the pay roll

Characters in Complete Font

A B C D E F G H I J K L M
N O P Q R S T U V W X
Y Z & $ 1 2 3 4 5 6 7 8 9 0
a b c d e f g h i j k l m n o p q
r s t u v w x y z ff fi fl ffi ffl ct
¶ ℰ . , - ' : ; ! ?

SMALL CAPS from 6 to 18 Point, and Oldstyle Figures
1234567890 in all sizes, are put up in separate fonts and furnished
only when specially ordered

Goudy was drawn to letters almost from the start. There is the story of his decorating the local Sunday School with Bible texts made up of letters cut from colored paper and pasted to the walls. Goudy said that he cut out over three thousand letters!

Goudy also tried his hand at sign painting in his youth. His first job is said to have been the local baker's new wagon. Goudy took great pains to make each letter of an equal width, and at an equal distance from each other. Thus the passion for typography, if not its principles, began to develop early.

Goudy's early employment was as a bookkeeper, but his mind was on letters. It was, therefore, natural that he and a friend started a private press. The Camelot Press of Chicago opened in 1895, with the goal of printing attractive advertising. Unfortunately, it did not last long.

GOUDY HARD AT WORK

## CAMELOT LIVES ON

In 1897, Goudy drew his first alphabet and submitted it to the Dickinson Type Foundry in Boston. He modestly asked for five dollars as a design commission and was quite surprised when he received a check for ten. Many decades later, the Compugraphic Corporation, in search of an old alphabet to test their newly purchased Ikarus system, chose Goudy's first design. Because of Compugraphic's search, Goudy's first typeface, Camelot, is still in use today—and is available in considerably more weights than Goudy would have envisioned.

Goudy's early ten dollar success encouraged him to devote more time to lettering. Several other alphabets were sold. Most were of the advertising display variety, and a few are still used occasionally; Pabst Roman, created for the brewery, and Powell, drawn for a major Chicago department store, are typical.

In 1903, Goudy and Will Ransom established the Village Press in Park Ridge, Illinois. Bertha Goudy joined her husband's and his friend's venture, and set the type for most of the books published at the press.

A year later the press was moved to Hingham, Massachusetts. William Dwiggins (who studied under Goudy in Chicago) and his wife, moved to Hingham shortly after Goudy did, to share in the work. When Goudy moved the Village Press once again, two years later, Dwiggins stayed on in the Boston area. He had found his home.

The Village Press finally settled in New York City, where it operated for two years before it burned.

In 1907, the Lanston Monotype Machine Company commissioned their first typeface from Goudy. The design was created for the advertising of a new New York department store: Gimbels. The finished design is a delicate face, based on French Old Style character traits. While many do not feel it is one of Goudy's better designs, it was his first to find general acceptance. The design came to be known as Monotype 38E.

Goudy eventually became the art director of Lanston Monotype Machine Company, which made his work widely available. Garamond, Kennerley, Italian Old Style, and Deepdene were released by Lanston Monotype.

In 1925, Goudy opened his own type foundry, something no type designer had done since the eighteenth century. For the next fourteen years Goudy worked out of the old mill on his property near Marlborough, New York. The matrices for his designs were originally cut by Robert Weibking; but when he died after two years of collaboration, Goudy undertook the unprecedented; at the age of 62 he secured the necessary equipment and learned the difficult art of engraving. Never before in the history of the graphic arts had a type designer owned and operated the machinery necessary to translate typeface designs into type. The first face created entirely by Goudy was Companion Old Style.

## TYPOGRAPHIC ENDURANCE —GOUDY STYLE

It is a testimony to Goudy's ability that so many of his designs are in active use today. Kennerley is available from virtually every supplier of graphic arts equipment. Goudy Old Style is a modern classic. Italian Old Style, National Old Style, Garamont, Deepdene, and even

Goudy Sans are still available on photo and digital composition equipment. Copperplate Gothic which was American Type Founder's all-time best-seller, and is still used for business cards and stationery, was a Goudy design. And finally ITC Berkeley Oldstyle, released by ITC in 1983, is based on Goudy's University of California Oldstyle.

Goudy's typefaces, according to one critic, are "beautiful because they are simple; they are dignified, sturdy, honest and strong." His faces stand up well whether they are used in display headlines or massed on a book page.

To the end of his 82 years, Goudy found pleasure in his work. He had the courage and the drive to do precisely what he wanted, in the way he wished. If people used and purchased his faces, that was fine. If they did not, he kept right on —empty pockets or not.

## THE COURAGEOUS PARTNER

Perhaps Goudy was able to do so much, to design so many faces, to create so much beautiful typography because he did not work alone: Bertha, his wife, was

AAABCDEFGHIJKLMNOPQ
RRSSTTUVWXYZ&.,';:!?-
aabcdeefghijklmnopqrstu
vwxyzfifffffiflffl$1234567890

Speaking of earlier types, Goudy says: The old fellows stole all of our best ideas.

GOUDY'S ONLY SANS

Pabst Italic

10 Point  16 A 38 a  
CONTENTMENT  
Many inhabitants of this town feel greatly relieved because income taxes were not increased as expected

8 Point  21 A 42 a  
DIFFERENT MOTIVES  
Poetry is the frolic of invention, the great dance of words, and the harmony of sound. Oratory is a judicious delivery of arguments

6 Point  22 A 49 a  
ENVIRONMENT PLEASED  
Meandering brooklets and autumnal coloring allure the traveler; mountain scenery and secluded homesteads offer rest and tranquillity for philosophers

18 Point  9 A 16 a  
DISGUISE  
Reporter finds legal document

14 Point  12 A 26 a  
LECTURING  
Medieval customs amaze bright youth

12 Point  16 A 35 a  
INSTRUCTIVE  
Political debate proves delightfully interesting

72 Point  3 A 4 a  
Stub

60 Point  3 A 4 a  
Eight

48 Point  3 A 6 a  
Helped

42 Point  4 A 6 a  
Nymph

36 Point  5 A 7 a  
MUSK  
Liquidate

30 Point  5 A 7 a  
DOZING  
Replenished

24 Point  6 A 10 a  
SHOCKED  
Quick Indians

Characters in Complete Font

A B C D E F G H I
J K L M N O P Q R
S T U V W X Y Z &
$ 1 2 3 4 5 6 7 8 9 0
a b c d e f g h i j k l
m n o p q r s t u v w
x y z ff fi fl ffi ffl Qu
. , - ' : ; ! ?

The following Special Characters are supplied with all fonts from 6 to 14 point inclusive. They are sold in separate fonts from 18 to 72 point inclusive and furnished only when specially ordered.

A B D G M N P R T

PABST ITALIC, COMPANION TO THE ROMAN ORIGINALLY
CREATED FOR THE PABST BREWERY IN CHICAGO

ABCDEFGHIJKL
MNOPQRSTUVW
XYZ&ÆŒ:,';:!?-
fi ff ffi fl ffl
abcdefghijklmnopqrs
tuvwxyzæœ£$123456
7890
Speaking of earlier types,
Goudy says: The old fellows
stole all of our best ideas:

TYPEFACE DESIGNED FOR GIMBELS DEPARTMENT STORE

✠ Certificate of Honor Dgpsy

MARLBOROUGH TEXT, GOUDY'S LAST
TYPE DESIGN

almost always at his side. It would be difficult to estimate the importance of the part Bertha Goudy played in the life and work of her husband. From Fred, and from the Goudy's many friends, we learned that her influence was vast. Goudy himself said, "Bertha has aided and encouraged me with constant devotion for over thirty-five years, and without her help I should not have accomplished a tithe of what I have been privileged to perform. She has been the staff that I have leaned upon so many times, the courageous partner who smiled and gritted her teeth when we had no funds, the one who renewed my faith and revived my spirits when they sagged so often. In the many activities of the Press her work ranks in actual accomplishment above my own. I could not, probably would not, have attempted the details of type composition for which she is, in fact, celebrated."

As a designer, Frederic Goudy displayed originality and great technical skill. As a printer, he developed a distinct personal style. First and foremost, Goudy realized that type design is not the rendering of individual letters, but the creation of the most versatile form of visual communication. He mastered all the intricacies of type manufacture to ensure that his intentions as a designer were translated into a communications tool.

In an age of electronic and highly sophisticated typesetting, the most successful designers are those who emulate Goudy's drive and ambition. They delve deeply into the technical problems of modern printing and press the technicians to provide the most versatile and effective instruments to compose typography.

# Morris Fuller Benton

## 1872–1948

When the greats of American type design are discussed, some names are inevitably brought up: Frederic Goudy, Oz Cooper, Ed Benguiat, William Dwiggins.

Rarely is the name Morris Fuller Benton mentioned. Yet he belongs in the company of these other greats. He was responsible for more faces than Frederic Goudy, and his work was issued by one of the most influential companies in American typographic history.

Who was Morris Fuller Benton? He has been called the unknown father of American typeface design. A list of just a few of his designs shows the magnitude of this man's contribution:

Century Schoolbook

Cheltenham

Franklin Gothic

Stymie

News Gothic

Century Oldstyle

Hobo

Broadway

Alternate Gothic No. 2

Even seven faces usually attributed to Goudy are the result of Benton's work. He made typefaces for handset foundry type over 70 years ago, and his designs live on, transcending typographic trends and technological developments.

## LIKE FATHER, LIKE SON

It was natural that Benton be involved with type in one way or another. His father, Linn Boyd Benton, invented the matrix cutting machine and was one of the founding directors of the American Type Founders (AFT) Company. Like many small boys, Benton wanted to grow up to be like his father, and spent many of his free hours at the elder Benton's foundry. In fact, the younger Benton's first job was working under his father at ATF.

Like the two Bentons, ATF also holds a special place in the history of our industry. The company was formed as a merger of the major independent type founders operating within the United States in the late 1800s. ATF then went on to become one of the most influential forces in the typesetting and printing industry during the first half of this century —but that is another story.

Although his greatest achievements were in typeface development, Benton wasn't trained to be an artist or designer. He was educated as a mechanical engineer and was first hired in that capacity at ATF. This mechanical interest and aptitude reflected itself in almost all aspects of Benton's life. Many of his children's toys were made by him and his father, and his love for one of the mechanical marvels of his age, the automobile, is well documented. The Bentons' first family car was a Stanley Steamer, a unique and exotic piece of machinery even by today's standards.

Perhaps his employers felt that his mechanical ability endowed Benton with a systematic, organized mind. Or perhaps the young engineer displayed a creative ability. Possibly he just poked his head into his father's office at the right moment. For whatever reason, ATF reassigned Benton early in his career from his engineering duties to typeface development. This simple corporate personnel change has benefited the typographic industry for decades.

CENTURY SCHOOLBOOK
CHELTENHAM
**FRANKLIN GOTHIC**
STYMIE
NEWS GOTHIC
CENTURY OLDSTYLE
HOBO
BROADWAY
ALTERNATE GOTHIC NO. 2
ITC BENGUIAT GOTHIC
BABY TEETH
ITC AMERICAN TYPEWRITER

A FEW BENTON TYPE FAMILIES

## FORMATIBLE TASKS

It became Benton's task to standardize and consolidate the thousands of type matrices that were acquired when ATF was formed. With his new responsibility came a raise, and two major problems.

First, the point system for sizing type was a very recent concept. Only a few of the ATF foundries had adopted it at the time of the merger. Most of the acquired faces went back to old standards that were at best imprecise, and often conflicting. Second, and more important to the future of type design, there was a tremendous amount of typeface duplication among the ATF foundries. To further complicate matters, the offerings from each foundry were frequently inconsistent in family size, weight designations, and design variations.

As a result of the process of sorting out the typographic mess confronting him, Benton firmly established the concept of typeface families and family development. Ultimately, the proliferation of this concept improved typographic communication. Today we benefit from many carefully conceived typeface families that provide typographers and type specifiers with designs that bring harmony, continuity, and structure to graphic communication. Benton created order out of chaos for ATF and gave the typographic industry the ability for efficient communication. This was the first of Benton's typographic successes. Many more were to follow—in the form of typeface designs.

As a typeface designer, Benton brought two seemingly diverse qualities to his work. He was both artist and pragmatist. His typefaces were almost always the combined product of artistic inspiration and organized, systematic research. Added to this was his deep and enthusiastic love of the letterform. The results can be seen in all his designs.

## UNCOMMON DIVERSITY

There is also a diversity of style found in Benton's work that is uncommon among typeface designers. The range of his creations extends from the elegant designs of Sterling and Bulmer to the structured faces of Franklin Gothic and Stymie. He successfully created blackletter faces like Wedding Text and Cloister Black, and was also perfectly capable of creating scripts such as Ad and Typo Script. Souvenir is generally considered to be friendly. Phenix could be called austere, and Hobo and Motto show a sense of humor.

To see the humor and vitality in Benton's work, one need only look at the designs of Roycroft, Hobo, Broadway, or Novel Gothic. Clearly, someone with a sense of humor created these typefaces. In addition, the designs have a warm and friendly look; and while they may not be considered particularly graceful or elegant, they have a design refinement seldom found in novelty type styles. Perhaps this is why they have survived the test of time better than many other, similar faces. All are currently used by typographic communicators.

Roycroft and Hobo are well over 70 years old, yet they are both available and used today—in phototype, on dry transfer sheets, and even in digital form—Hobo by its original name, Roycroft as ITC Gorilla. Not to be overshadowed, Novel Gothic and Broadway are still versatile headline faces seen in a variety of advertising.

## THE MOST FAMOUS FUNNY FACE

Souvenir was a Benton design that showed his ability to create a friendly design that went beyond the limits of headline and display typography. Souvenir, however, unlike many Benton designs, was not an instant success. As friendly as Souvenir is accredited to be, it wasn't very popular when first issued. Released as a single weight, with no italic, in 1914, its only major showing appeared in the ATF specimen book. Very little of Souvenir was sold and ATF never showed it again. That probably would have been

ABCDEFGHI
JKLMNOPQR
STUVWXYZ&$
1 2 3 4 5 6 7 8 9 0
abcdefgh
ijklmnopq
rstuvwxyz
.,-:;!?'()

STYMIE

Written in Italian in the year 1422, translated into French by Raoul Georges a year later, and now done in English by John Watson and Mary Grover Sinclair MCMXXIV

CLOISTER BLACK

*Informal Dance*

*Given for the benefit of the Metropolitan Welfare League*
*Society of Philanthropists*

*Friday Evening, April 4th*
*Eight thirty o'clock*

*Ball Room, Hotel Walheim, Independence Square*
*Providence, Rhode Island*

TYPO SLOPE

ABCDEFGHIJKL
MNOPQRSTUVWXYZ &
1234567890
!?$:;"",,.

PHENIX

the end of Souvenir, if it hadn't been for Ed Benguiat. In 1971, he revived the design as ITC Souvenir. In the process he developed three additional weights to fill out the family and created the italic designs that now complement the roman. Today this friendliest of Benton's designs is used on all kinds of composing equipment—from sophisticated laser typesetters used by advertising typographers to on-demand publishing systems found in the office environment.

If Benton were remembered for his friendly, warm, sometimes funny designs, it would be an important legacy to the tradition of American typeface design. Typefaces like Ed Benguiat's ITC Benguiat Gothic, Milton Glaser's Baby Teeth, and ITC American Typewriter follow in its tradition. Benton did more.

## CLASSIC REVIVALS

He also made research and a respect for typographic tradition part of his development programs. Cloister Oldstyle is a perfect example. It is based on the roman design of Nicolas Jenson which was first used in 1470. Benton's interpretation of the original is the product of extensive research into Jenson's work. The result is one of the finest examples of traditional typeface design. Many typefaces have been based on Jenson's original designs—both before and after Benton's effort—but authorities generally agree that Cloister Oldstyle is one of the most successful. And since Jenson lived before italic type was introduced, Benton had to turn to other sources for the design of Cloister Oldstyle Italic. For this design Benton also based his work on the results of research. Cloister Italic was derived from a careful study of the first italic letters developed in the early 1500s. Not only are Cloister Oldstyle and Cloister Oldstyle Italic exceptional examples of reviving a past master's work, the two designs were also successfully melded into a cohesive typographic unit. The Cloister Oldstyle family is a classic example of something

ABCDEFGHIJ
KLMMNOPQRR
STUVWXYZ&
$1234567890
aabcdefghhi
jklmmnnopq
rsttuuvwxyz
fi fl The ct f sh si fl st

ROYCROFT

ABCDEFGHIJKLM
NOPQRSTUVWXYZ&
abcdefghijklm
nopqrstuvwxyz
1234567890

NOVEL GOTHIC

WANDELING
AUTO TIRES

Manufactured to satisfy the natural demand for service and for mileage. two important elements that determine the very life of a tire. Wandeling tires give you service of a kind that is peculiarly satisfying. with unusual freedom from troubles.

Manufactured by the

WANDELING TIRE COMPANY
CHICAGO. ILLINOIS

HOBO

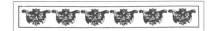

Recital of
## Romantic Italian Music
Given by
MR. JOHN M. LIVERMORE
Under the auspices and direction of the Sophomore
Class of Bellwood University
November twenty-seventh at eight-thirty
Music Hall

This is the first of a series of six recitals to be given by Mr. Livermore during the winter

ABCDEFGHIJKLMNOPQRSTUVWXYZ
**ABCDEFGHIJKLMNOPQRSTUVWXYZ**
**ABCDEFGHIJKLMNOPQRSTUVWXYZ**
**ABCDEFGHIJKLMNOPQRSTUVWXYZ**
*ABCDEFGHIJKLMNOPQRSTUVWXYZ*
*ABCDEFGHIJKLMNOPQRSTUVWXYZ*
*ABCDEFGHIJKLMNOPQRSTUVWXYZ*
*ABCDEFGHIJKLMNOPQRSTUVWXYZ*

SOUVENIR

A B C D E F G H
I J K L M N O
P Q R R S T T
U V W X Y Z &
$ 1 2 3 4 5 6 7 8 9 0
a b c d e f g h i j
k l m n o p q r s t
u v w x y z ff fi fl
ffi ffl Qu & ( ) [ ]

CLOISTER OLDSTYLE

*A A B B C C D D E*
*E F G G H I J Jʒ K*
*L M M N N O P*
*P Q R R S T T U*
*V U W X Y Y Z &*
*$ 1 2 3 4 5 6 7 8 9 0*
*a b c d e f g h i j*
*k k l m n o p q r s t*
*u v v w w x y z ff fi*
*fl ffi ffl Qu & st ( ) [ ]*

CLOISTER OLDSTYLE ITALIC

in which the total unit is greater than the sum of its parts.

Several of Benton's designs were also re-creations of classic typestyles revived to be current with contemporary typesetting and typographic standards. His Bodoni and Garamond have become two of the most successful revivals in typographic history. While both design programs involved extensive research into the original masters' typefaces and design philosophy, neither is just a copy. They are careful interpretations of the original work. In the case of Bodoni, Benton tried to choose the best qualities from the 18 variations of Bodoni created and used by their originator. Benton must have made the correct decisions, because his version of Bodoni has become the American standard for this style. The same is true of his Garamond, which was further refined in 1976 by Tony Stan, when it provided much of the basis for the development of ITC Garamond.

Benton's research into eyesight and reading comprehension led to the development of Century Schoolbook. A typeface originally conceived (as the name implies) for the setting of schoolbooks, Benton's results were so successful that the design has become a standard for text typography. In fact, Benton's Century Schoolbook has provided the foundation for virtually every "legibility" typeface design developed since its introduction. If for no other reason, Morris Fuller Benton should be remembered for his contribution to the development of high-legibility typeface designs.

Today Century Schoolbook is available, in one form or another, from every manufacturer of typographic composing equipment. It has become a typographic requirement. As a further extension of this style, many of its design traits have been combined with another Benton design, Century Expanded, to create ITC Century.

It was Benton's dedication to aiding the typographic communicator that prompted the development of one of the first systematically designed sans serif

GARAMOND

A RIDE IN THE CARS

Evelyn cars ride one these ticket two aboard New York all Donald

*Characters.* MAY, GRACE, EVELYN, GEORGE, DONALD, JACK, WILL, FRANK, TICKET MAN

(Arrange chairs for a train of cars, and have one chair with a table or a desk for a ticket office. Let the children make tickets for busy work)

DONALD. Do you wish to ride in my cars?

EVELYN. Yes, thank you. I wish to ride in your cars.

CENTURY SCHOOLBOOK

CENTURY EXPANDED
A TYPE WITHOUT HAIRLINES

Unsurpassed for use in textbooks, directories, catalogues and commercial work in general

AMERICAN TYPE FOUNDERS COMPANY, *Maker*

CENTURY EXPANDED

A B C D E F G H I
J K L M N O P Q R S
T U V W X Y Z & $
1 2 3 4 5 6 7 8 9 0
a b c d e f g h i j k l
m n o p q r s t u v w
x y z . , - ' : ; ! ?

ALTERNATE GOTHIC

UNIVERS

typeface families: Alternate Gothic. The original intention for the Alternate Gothic family was to aid the printer in setting justified lines of copy. Before automatic justification, making multiple lines of typography end flush left and right was a difficult task that involved inserting space, by hand, between each word, or even between every letter within a line. Benton's idea was to create a series of typefaces that had the same optical stroke width, but different proportional character width. The typographer could use the condensed design to pack a larger number of words or characters into a line, and the expanded design to help fill out otherwise short lines.

Whether or not the Alternate Gothic family was used for its original intention is not well documented; but typographers did purchase enough of the design to make it one of the most successful sans serif type styles of the time. And like so many other Benton creations, Alternate Gothic is still produced and used today. But what is more important, it was the first systematically planned, carefully organized sans serif typeface family.

Type families like Univers, Unica, and Gerstner Program follow in its tradition.

## MAKING AN IMPACT

Benton spent his life creating typeface designs—more than most, better than most. We reap the benefits.

His contributions to American typography and typeface design were all encompassing, and the body of his work is unparalleled. The majority of the faces he created live on today, surviving trends in typographic fashion and technological changes in type composition. But what is more important, Benton's designs have become the foundation for typeface design in the United States. The tradition of combining the pursuit of excellence with a sense of humor, and maintaining classic design attributes in the search for originality began with the work of Morris Fuller Benton. He made a major impact on current typographic communication and, in doing so, accomplished what most designers achieve only in their dreams.

# Rudolf Koch
1876–1934

Rudolf Koch believed that, in the creation of a typeface, the work of the type designer and that of the punch cutter were inseparable and of absolute equal value. While an artist and designer first, Koch yearned to try his hand at punch cutting.

"Seven years were necessary," he wrote, "before I had the courage to do this." But, with some obvious anxiety, Koch began working on Neuland, a typeface cut directly in metal—with virtually no preliminary drawings. When the first proofs were shown to Dr. Klingspor, the owner of the foundry that employed Koch, the immediate response was "abominable, horrible, unbearably ugly! . . . but by all means go ahead."

## THE ARTIST AND THE BUSINESSMAN

To this day, Neuland is not considered a particularly practical, useful, or attractive typeface. Dr. Klingspor's initial opinion has also been endorsed by a majority of the typophiles who have since critiqued the Neuland type. The obvious question is, Why was Koch encouraged to continue work on the type and why was it eventually released? The answer is that Dr. Klingspor, in addition to being a good businessman, valued artistic expression and was wise enough to know that artists must be allowed the freedom to experiment—and (from time to time) to fail. He realized that Koch was a rare blend of artist and craftsman, and that both aspects of his personality required support and encouragement.

Type design was but one of Koch's artistic outlets. In addition, he was a calligrapher, illustrator, poet, and designer of books and tapestries. This small, almost odd-looking man left a very large, and exceptionally beautiful, impression on the early 20th-century graphic arts. While the diversity of his output was extensive, encompassing many forms of artistic expression, letters were the unifying theme of all his work. Koch, first and always, considered himself a lettering artist.

"Lettering," he once wrote, "gives me the purest and greatest pleasure, and on countless occasions in my life it has been to me what song is to the singer, painting to the painter, a cheer to the joyous, and a sigh to the afflicted. To me it is the happiest and most perfect expression of my life."

## ARTIST AND EDUCATOR

Throughout history the relatively few special artists who compounded their contribution were those who also were teachers. Koch was such an artist. He once wrote to a friend, "I feel sorry for the poor art students. . . . I am certainly no organizer, but if I had a workshop I know that I could help at least a few of them. . . . To be surrounded by just a few honest and serious students, to be their helper and leader, that would please me. . . ."

Koch eventually got his wish. The Offenbach School of Art, near where he worked, provided him with a long, narrow room directly under the school roof. The makeshift classroom's walls were slanted, and windows (which one had to climb on a table to see out of) were only on one side. The cramped workspace had no stove or other source of heat, and the attic windows provided little ventilation. As a result, Koch's small band of students sweltered in the summer heat and were forced to wear heavy clothing to class in the winter. But Koch was satisfied—even happy—teaching in these simple surroundings.

Koch worked his whole life in Germany, during the first part of the century. To some degree this was an unfortunate circumstance for the international graphic communications community. Fraktur, or German gothic types, were the dominant type styles used in Germany at the time. As a result, much of Koch's creative efforts were directed toward designing those beautiful, but today, little-used styles.

As with most of Koch's work, his Frakturs were not conservative in design;

Die Kunst ist ein ernsthaftes Geschäft, am ernsthaftesten, wenn sie sich mit edlen heiligen Gegenständen beschäftigt; der Künstler aber steht über der Kunst und dem Gegenstande: über jener, da er sie zu seinen Zwecken braucht, über diesem, weil er ihn nach eigner Weise behandelt.

KOCH'S WILHELM KINGSPOR SCHRIFT

A DECORATIVE KOCH ALPHABET

they tended to be explorations of the design envelope.

At the turn of the century, German printers, typographers, and publishers became dissatisfied with the gothic types that had prevailed since Gutenberg's first work. They had a desire for simpler type—more like the roman designs used in the rest of western Europe. Encouraged by this and influenced by the "Jugendstil," or art nouveau, German type designers began to experiment with new and simpler letter shapes.

## BRITISH INFLUENCE ON A GERMAN ARTIST

It is interesting that the work of a British designer, William Morris, helped to define this attitude. His Troy type of 1892 was a melding of gothic and roman letterforms. Troy was, at best, a controversial design in Britain. But it did find its way to the United States, when the American Type Founders released their own version of the style, under the name Satanik. The design wasn't very popular in the United States either, but it was eventually ordered by a number of German printers, who began to use the face with zeal. Within a short time, Satanik, and various appropriated similar designs, became one of the most used typefaces in Germany.

Much of Koch's work with German gothic letterforms was an exploration of gothic and roman letter shapes based on the foundation laid by Satanik. In fact, the distinctive lowercase "g", which is almost a trademark of Koch's designs, can trace its heritage to the Troy types of William Morris.

His first roman type was released as "Koch-Antiqua" in Germany; throughout the rest of Europe it became known as "Locarno", and in the United States it was for some reason given the name "Eve." Locarno is the name that stuck. The roman was first released in 1922, followed by an italic a year later, and the bold a year after that.

As with most of Koch's alphabet designs, the hand of the artist is readily apparent in Locarno. This is clearly a type best suited to display and ephemeral applications—a typeface of obvious personality. Character strokes, while true to the capabilities of a broad brush, have unusual weight stress. Ascending strokes are quite heavy on top and taper to delicate bases. If anything, this is the very opposite of a normal ascending character stroke. Locarno also has a great diversity in character proportions. The first appearance of Koch's distinctive lowercase "g" is also found here.

In a short time, the design began to be used throughout Europe and continued in use for several years. Its popularity was echoed in America, when ATF released Rivoli, a close copy of Koch's original design.

Now, after several decades of rest, Koch's first roman has been updated and

ABCDEFGHIJKLMNOPQRSTUVWXYZ

ORIGINAL NEULAND (KINGSPOR 1923)

revived by Colin Brignall of Letraset Ltd. Brignall's main objective was to revise some of the characteristics of the original face without losing its distinctive personality. As a result, many subtle, and a few not-so-subtle, changes were made to the basic design. An increased x-height, improved serif design for digital typesetting, and an evening of the capital proportions are the most prevalent design modifications. While the original Locarno is no longer offered, this new Letraset design is being made available through a number of typesetting equipment suppliers.

## THE UNPOPULAR CHOICE

One year after the release of Locarno, in 1923, Koch's Neuland was announced. The project was primarily an experiment on his part—a chance to test, in Koch's words, the "measure of freedom in the formation of characters which could not have been achieved by any other means." His goal was to create a type through the direct action of the engraving tools on metal—with no preliminary drawings or sketches. Koch felt that this method was (1) truer to the historical method for the way type was produced in the past, and (2) would provide him the opportunity to participate firsthand, in the total type design experience.

Virtually no one at the Klingspor type foundry was in favor of his new design. If it had been put to a vote, Neuland would never have seen the light of day. Artists and company owners, however, are not known for democratic attitudes when it comes to their personal preferences, so work proceeded without delay.

It is difficult to determine whether Koch's experiment has any practical value; in fact, some type critics would probably compare his effort to the old medical adage, "The operation was a success, but the patient died." While Neuland is a robust and distinctive design, it is not especially attractive, nor even very useful. Its realistic applications are quite limited.

And yet, when first released, the type was popular—so much so that a number of competitive foundries felt compelled to copy the design. It even made the transition from metal to phototype in the 1970s.

the quick brown fox jumps over the dog
**Cable Light (later redesigned and called Kabel) (Klingspor 1927–29)**

the quick brown fox jumps over the dog
**Cable Medium**

the quick brown fox jumps over the dog
**Cable Heavy**

ABCDEFGHIJKL
abcdefghijklmnop
**Marathon (Klingspor 1931)**

ABCDEFGHIJKL
abcdefghijklmno
**Wallau (Klingspor 1925–30)**

ABCDEFGHIJK
abcdefghijklmno
**Wallau Bold**

SEVERAL OF KOCH'S TYPEFACES

## KOCH'S MOST FAMOUS —AND POPULAR—DESIGN

The design of Kabel was the result of another experiment of sorts—an odd experiment for Koch, who prided himself on his calligraphic ability. In his words, "The task of creating a type with a pair of compasses and a straight edge has always attracted me. . . ."

In addition to Koch's desire for experimentation, Kabel was created for pragmatic reasons. In this design, Dr. Klingspor played more the role of businessman than art patron.

In the late 1920s, every other major German type foundry had either released, or was actively working on, a new kind of sans serif design based on geometric shapes. Ludwig and Mayer had already released Erbar, the Bauer foundry was developing Futura, and Berthold AG was busy working on Berthold Grotesque. To remain competitive, Klingspor would have to release a competing type.

While there is some confusion among type historians as to which came first—Koch's desire or Klingspor's need—the end result is not only exceptionally attractive and useful, it is also very different from those of its competitors. The reason is that, true to form, in the typeface design process, Koch's artistic personality took precedence over any geometric formula.

Although the specimen book that announced Kabel went to great lengths to explain the rationale behind the design and to prove its geometric heritage, a close look will reveal that the explanation and accompanying graphics are more window-dressing than design formula. It is obvious that Koch based his letter shapes and character proportions on artistic sensibilities and even, perhaps, on a creative whim or two. The close look at Kabel reveals many nongeometric influences. Its design traits can be traced to ancient Greek lapidary letters, Venetian oldstyle type designs, and, of course, calligraphy.

Kabel was successful when first released but was up against some stiff competition for market share. In an attempt to tone down some of the original idiosyncrasies (and perhaps gain more commercial success), Klingspor released a revised version of Kabel under the name of Neu Kabel. In this version, Koch's distinctive "a," "e," and "g" were much closer to the more popular Futura design.

Both Kabels obtained modest but sustained success as metal type. In the early 1970s, phototypesetting equipment manufacturers converted one or both faces into film fonts. Then, in 1976, ITC licensed the rights to the design and the name from Berthold AG, which at that time owned the typeface and released ITC Kabel as an updated and revived family. Since then, ITC Kabel has been made available on virtually every form of type imaging device, from dry-transfer lettering, to graphic arts typesetters, to modest resolution laser printers.

## A STRONG ARTISTIC PERSONALITY

In each of his typefaces Koch left his artistic thumbprint. His talent was not in creating anonymous, workhorse designs. Koch's faces were distinctive, vital, even a little flamboyant. He more than likely received a fair amount of criticism as a result. In fact, at one point he wrote, "People are always saying that I try to express my own personality in type design, but that is not at all true; on the contrary, I do my best to avoid such expressionism. Only I am not always successful."

Rudolf Koch was born in Nuremberg in 1876, the son of an unsuccessful sculptor who barely supported his family on small salary as chief of guards at the Bavarian Arts and Crafts Museum. Koch's father died at an early age, leaving his mother with only a small pension on which to raise her children.

At 16, a family friend, seeing that Koch faced an uncertain and probably

LOCARNO (ORIGINALLY PART OF
KOCH ANTIQUA SERIES)

bleak future with a public school education, took him into his factory as an apprentice engraver. Koch, however, felt his prospects there were bleaker than what would face him after a public education, and began to attend art school at night. Working 11 hours a day and attending art school after work was tedious, tiring, and draining on Koch's spirits. He stuck it out for several months, but eventually gave up hope that this was the correct path to success.

Overall, Koch's early career was pretty dismal. At one point, even his family regarded him as a hopeless failure. In his late twenties he was barely supporting himself and his new wife on the meager earnings of a freelance illustrator (although he confessed that he could neither draw nor paint) and as a part-time book designer.

Calligraphy became his career's saving grace. The turning point came one night while working at home. He began to imitate broad pen letterforms from a book illustration. Koch had no previous knowledge of type or calligraphy, but, as he wrote in his autobiography, there was character in his first stroke. For months he secretly practiced his new-found craft, afraid to show it to the world and face yet another failure.

Cautiously at first, he began to show the results of his effort. To Koch's surprise they weren't rejected. In fact, publishers began to hire his services on a regular basis!

In 1906 Koch read in a newspaper that the Klingspor type foundry was seeking a type designer. He saw this as a chance to both legitimize his craft and provide steady income for his family. Although fully expecting to be rejected, Koch applied for the position—and to his amazement was hired. Moving himself and his family to Offenbach, across the Main river from Frankfurt, Koch found the home and career that was to last the rest of his life.

## THE WAR'S EFFECT ON A GENTLE MAN

For eight years, Koch lead a tranquil and happy life, basking in peer acceptance and a good income. When World War I broke out, in spite of being over 40 and having a family of four children, Koch was called into service. There was no glory there for Koch; he never rose above the rank of private. In the infantry he fought long and bloody battles in France and Serbia, eventually to be wounded and hospitalized for several months.

Even though he tried to continue his calligraphy, there was no solace from his friendly letterforms during the war. Koch tells one story that seems typical. He was once in a rear area and ordered to paint street signs. A young soldier who was to help with the job disclosed that his father was the owner of a printing business. Koch, by way of making conversation, asked the young man if he knew anything about type. When the soldier emphatically said that he did, Koch showed him a newspaper printed in his own typeface. The young man was disturbed that he could not name the face, whereupon Koch told him that it was "Kochscrift"—one of his own designs.

The young man wouldn't believe Koch and declared that fine typefaces were drawn by famous professors who would never find themselves to be lowly privates in a dirty war. Koch recalled that he was so embarrassed that he did not know how to answer, and began to have serious doubts that he really had created that type!

Like many veterans, Koch returned home after the war a changed person. He became even more subdued and doubting of his abilities. Fortunately, he was surrounded by friends who cared for him and admired his work. He began designing type again, slowly at first, and expanded his classroom into a place of work and study.

TWO YEARS before the END OF the seventeenth

ORIGINAL LOCARNO BOLD

**New Locarno by Letraset**

ABCDEFGHIJKLMNOPQRSTUVWXYZÆØ
abcdefghijkklmnopqrstuvwxyzææøß1234567890 &?!£$%(.,;:)×«⁄-·˙˙°*
**Light**

ABCDEFGHIJKLMNOPQRSTUVWXYZÆØ
abcdefghijkklmnopqrstuvwxyzææøß1234567890 &?!£$%(.,;:)×«⁄-·˙˙°*
**Medium**

ABCDEFGHIJKLMNOPQRSTUVWXYZÆØ
abcdefghijkklmnopqrstuvwxyzææøß1234567890 &?!£$%(.,;:)×«⁄-·˙˙°*
**Bold**

ABCDEFGHIJKLMNOPQRSTUVWXYZÆØ
abcdefghijkklmnopqrstuvwxyzææøß1234567890 &?!£$%(.,;:)
**Extra Bold**

NEW LOCARNO BY LETRASET

After a while, his workshop flourished and visitors came from around the world to share in the experience. From Switzerland came Willi Baus and Imre Reiner. From Vienna came Victor Hammer. Joseph Blumenthal and Lydia and Waren Chappel came from the United States, and Stanley Morison and Francis Meynell from Great Britain. Berthold Wolpe, Fritz Kredel, and Henri Friedlaender came from surrounding Germany.

Calligraphy and lettering were their main interests, but carved inscriptions, tapestries, coins, metalwork, map making, bookbinding, and even church bells were part of the workshop's repertoire.

At the time of his death in 1934, Koch's workshop in Offenbach rivaled the creative output of the Bauhaus (on a somewhat smaller scale). But the oncoming war, and the lack of a creative focal point ended any chances of the workshop continuing for another generation. One by one the artists, designers, and students left.

## CONTRIBUTIONS OF AN ARTIST

Koch's contribution to our typographic heritage can be summed up as a number of well drawn typefaces still in use today. That, however, would be selling the man and his value short. Rudolf Koch should serve as an example to all designers of utilitarian tools: He did not let convention, technology, or lack of immediate success sway him from his goal of creating artistic, and to his mind, beautiful products. Koch was an artist, in the truest, highest meaning of the word. The typographic community has benefited from this man—through his work, and through his example.

*Oswald Cooper*

1879–1940

When George Jones, the distinguished type designer for Linotype back in the 1920s, visited Chicago on a business trip, he wanted to see everything and meet everyone associated with typography in that city. His guide rightly figured that a visit to a typical advertising typography studio would be of interest to Mr. Jones. The studio he chose was Bertsch and Cooper, the workplace of Oswald Cooper.

Mr. Jones's escort made somewhat casual introductions at Bertsch and Cooper prior to a half-hour tour of the business. As he left, Jones expressed thanks for the tour, but out on the street, he expressed deep disappointment:

"But I expected to meet Mr. Cooper, the famous Mr. Oswald Cooper who designs type—where is he today?"

"Good Lord, man," his guide said, "you've been talking with him for the last half-hour!"

"Oh, I'm so disappointed," Mr. Jones exclaimed. "Why didn't he tell me?"

Mr. Cooper was not long on personal pronouncements. Oswald B. Cooper ("Mr. Cooper" to most, "Oz" to some, and "Ozzie" to his closest friends) was reticent, humble, and almost excessively modest. He never sought acclaim and always credited the work of others over his own.

## On Everybody's List

Ask almost any student of typography to name the great American type designers, and Oz Cooper will be on the list. Ask the most seasoned typophile to list the types designed by Cooper, and few would get beyond two families. So why is this man, who so diligently avoided the limelight, who can only be remembered for designing a couple of typefaces, so well known to the typographic community? Probably for several reasons. First, his typeface Cooper Black was one of the most popular typefaces ever to be released in America up until that time. No single typeface, before or since, has made quite the impression on the graphic design community as Cooper Black. In addition, in spite of his preference for anonymity, Cooper's hand lettering and advertising design became the very visible cornerstone of what was to become the Midwest design style of the 1920s and 1930s. Had he never designed a typeface, Cooper's abundant and exceptional lettering would have been enough for him to be remembered. And finally, his friend and business partner, Fred Bertsch, worked very hard to promote Cooper and his skills.

In addition to being a graphic designer, lettering artist, and creator of typefaces, Oz Cooper was also a teacher—the best kind of teacher: He knew his craft intimately, was eager to share his knowledge and enthusiasm, and never limited his teaching to the classroom environment. Before he met Fred Bertsch and became a successful and well-known designer, Oz Cooper was an unrenowned instructor at Chicago's Frank Holme School of Illustration. The job didn't pay much (in fact, at times it didn't pay anything at all), but Cooper loved it.

Cooper's first exposure to the Frank Holme School was as a correspondence student from his home in Coffeyville, Kansas. After a couple of successful courses at an elementary level, Cooper moved to Chicago to attend class in person. His goal was to become a famous illustrator. He soon discovered, however, that once past the entry-level courses, his motivation and skill in the field of illustration took a nosedive. Cooper, himself, wrote that he was "just no good at drawing pictures."

## A Little Help from Fred

But Oz was, by this time, hooked on graphics, and in an attempt to find new direction for his sidetracked career, he took a sampling of virtually every course the school offered. He eventually ended up in a lettering class taught by Frederic Goudy. Here he found a wonderful teacher, and his new career path: Oz Cooper had discovered type. Cooper

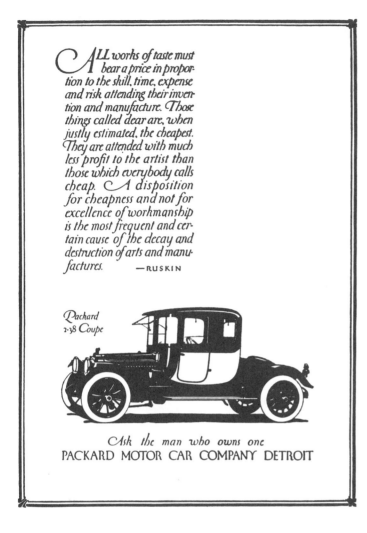

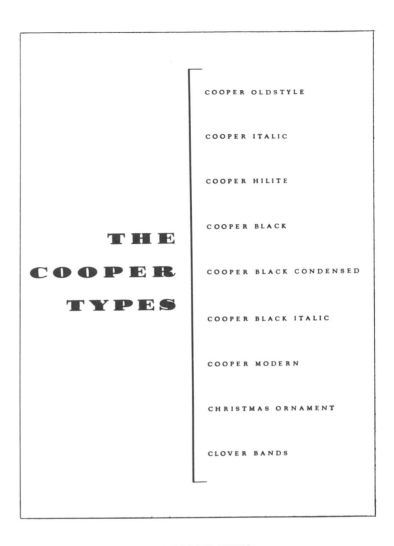

COOPER AD FOR THE PACKARD MOTOR CAR COMPANY          THE COOPER TYPES

studied diligently under Goudy, who, in Cooper's words, taught him "a thing or two about lettering." As Goudy's work as a type designer became more demanding, he was able to devote less time to the Frank Holme School. Undaunted, Cooper first began to study under the other educators at the school; then he moved on to what would be called "independent graduate work" in a more formal institution. Then he began to teach a class or two himself.

When Goudy left the Frank Holme School to devote full-time effort to type design, Cooper took over most of the typography and lettering classes. Eventually he assumed the title of Director of the Correspondence School of Typography. Oz liked teaching and his position at the Frank Holme school, and probably

would have stayed there for many years had not personal and financial tragedies struck the institution.

## Excellent
## Educators, But . . .

The directors of the Frank Holme School were artists and designers first, educators second, and business executives third. As a result, classes were stimulating, and course material had real-world relevance—but nobody watched the bottom line. Finally, one day a bank notice provided a hint that all was not well in the financial department. At this point, Fred Goudy, because he had some earlier experience as an accountant, was called on to try to bal-

COOPER-DESIGNED TYPE
ORNAMENTS

ance the school's books. He believed that a modest profit was in the offing.

The bank didn't agree. When a qualified accountant was called in, it became clear that the school was in debt— very much in debt.

Instructors began to leave the school for more stable employment, enrollment dropped, and even the school's founder was forced to leave because of poor health. Within a few months, nothing was left but a handful of teachers and students, a serious commitment to those who studied through correspondence, and an ever-growing debt.

Then Frank Holme died, and Oz Cooper was alone.

## IT SEEMED LIKE A GOOD IDEA AT THE TIME

One benefit of taking a correspondence course through the Frank Holme School was that students were allowed to drop out of the program and return at any time they wished to resume their studies. To enable this, full tuition was due upon entry to the school. This concept, which seemed like a good idea while the school prospered, suddenly turned sour and left hundreds of correspondence students with holes in their bank accounts—and no education to show for it.

Oz Cooper single-handedly took on the school's obligation to those students. Working without pay, he faithfully and conscientiously sent out assignments and provided in-depth critiques to the students.

The story is even told that, 17 years after the school closed, two nuns came to Cooper's studio. They had searched out Cooper on behalf of an invalid patient who, many years before, had begun but didn't finish a Frank Holme correspondence course in typography and lettering. They produced a yellowed contract and beseeched Mr. Cooper to once again take the student on. Oz willingly honored the contract.

But Cooper's commitment to education did not stop at honoring correspondence school contracts. The young and inexperienced designers in his studio often benefited from Mr. Cooper's "lessons." There was no trick of lettering that Oz declined to share, no hint, no production or design guideline that he didn't take time to explain. Those who worked with Oz Cooper not only benefited from their employment in Chicago's most creative and fashionable design firm, they also received free tutoring from Chicago's hottest lettering artist and graphic designer.

## OPPOSITES ATTRACT

While teaching at the Frank Holme School, Cooper met a young man who was to become a friend, a lifelong business partner, and his biggest fan. Fred Bertsch ran an art service next door to the Holme School. Bertsch was as flamboyant and energetic as Cooper was unpretentious and methodical. Bertsch was the consummate salesman, Cooper the reticent craftsman. Hardly a more contrasting pair of personalities could have existed. And yet, they became close friends. When Bertsch's business associates left in 1904 to find a more tranquil work environment, he persuaded Oz Cooper to become his partner. Bertsch & Cooper was formed with the intention of providing the new business associates with a career based on their continued love of type and typography. A full-service type shop was the goal. But since type cost money, a commodity they happened to have in very short supply, the partners were forced to turn to advertising design and hand lettering until they could fulfill their dream.

Cooper did the lettering and much of the design, while Bertsch's primary responsibility was to bring in business. The two worked hard. As they gained recognition for their small jobs, bigger accounts came in. Soon Bertsch & Cooper was doing entire campaigns for many national accounts, including the Packard

Motor Car Company and Anheuser-Busch Breweries.

The vigorous character of Cooper's lettering and the freshness of his design style soon set his work apart from others of his time. In addition to the visual arts, Cooper also displayed a talent for copywriting. Many an ad profited not only from Oz's design and lettering ability, but also from his clear text laced with just a hint of dry Midwestern humor. Cooper clearly left his mark on the advertising of the early 20th century. In fact, his influence in advertising and graphic design was far greater than that of many better known artists and designers.

Entirely unself-seeking, Cooper preferred an almost cloistered life, his prominence being gained almost entirely through the sheer power of his work. Well, almost: Fred Bertsch devoted as much of his time to selling Oz as he did to selling the studio. (One was probably good for the other.) As a result, the work of Oz Cooper became famous even though the man remained out of public view.

## Finally Fonts

As Cooper's reputation grew, the partnership prospered, and at long last, in 1914, the dream of a type shop became a reality. Fonts of type and proofing equipment were purchased, a production staff hired, and even a manager for the new Typography Department was put on the Bertsch & Cooper payroll. Then, because they were able to take on more complete jobs, and because the demand on Cooper's time became more than he could handle (despite his working late nights and most weekends), it became necessary to expand the design department. Designers and production artists were hired, and later illustrators were added to the staff. Within a relatively short period of time, from when typography was first added to the list of Bertsch & Cooper services, the small two-man operation became one of

Chicago's busiest and most sought-after design and advertising agencies.

## Then There Was Type

Although he didn't design any typefaces until he was near middle age, it is his typefaces for which Oz Cooper is most remembered—well, one typeface anyway. Unfortunately, when it comes to identifying Oz Cooper's accomplishments as a type designer, few are able to expand the list much beyond Cooper Black. While not nearly as prolific as Frederic Goudy or William Dwiggins, Oswald Cooper created considerably more than just one design.

Actually, someone else drew Cooper's first typeface design. The Bertsch & Cooper design studio eventually became a full-service shop providing concept, design, copywriting, and (when a suitable type design was not available) hand lettering. In the early part of this century, the Packard Motor Car Company took advantage of all these services. The ads were highly successful and were in part made distinctive by the custom lettering Cooper did for all of them. Morris Fuller Benton at American Type Founders was also impressed by these ads, so impressed that he had one of his staff artists develop a typeface based on the hand lettering used in them. The completed design—coincidentally named "Packard"—was released by ATF in 1913.

This could have been just one more short chapter in the long history of typeface piracy, but fortunately Morris Benton was a man of ethics. When he learned that Mr. Cooper had drawn the original letterforms used in the Packard ads, he immediately took steps to have him paid for the design.

Cooper's second typeface (or the first to be drawn completely by him) also grew out of his hand lettering. By 1918, Cooper's work had become a distinctive, and very popular, lettering style.

ATA LOGOTYPE DESIGNED BY OZ COOPER

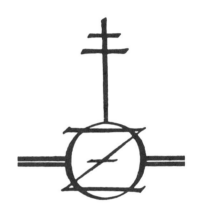

OZ COOPER'S OWN LOGO

_designers_

CALLIGRAPHY BY COOPER

## THE RELUCTANT DESIGNER

Hoping to cash in on an obviously popular graphic trend, the Barnhart Brothers & Spindler (BB&S) Type Foundry approached Cooper with a proposal to design a complete family of types based on his lettering. At first, Cooper wasn't too keen about the idea. After all, he wasn't a type designer; he was a lettering artist— and a busy one at that. Fred Bertsch, however, saw the opportunity to gain more exposure for Ozzie's work and to further promote the Bertsch & Cooper studio. Bertsch cajoled and Cooper wavered; Bertsch prodded and Cooper surrendered.

The project started with the design of the basic roman version of the family. Completed in 1918, the design was called simply "Cooper." The face was loosely based on oldstyle letterforms, but both BB&S and Cooper resisted calling the face "Cooper Oldstyle." The former resisted because they hoped to get an additional design or two out of Cooper and were saving the name for one of those. And the latter resisted because he knew type as well as hand lettering and was well aware that this endeavor was not a true oldstyle design, but more a caricature of the traditional type.

Cooper was released somewhat carefully in just a few point sizes as an advertising display face. (The face they really wanted to spend their big promotional dollars on was a bold design that was to be more in keeping with Cooper's hand-drawn headlines.) Success for Cooper's first face was only modest. But in all fairness, it would have been difficult for a type that was essentially a text design and available only in display sizes, to be much of a hit.

## SUPER TYPE

Next came Cooper Black. This is, arguably, the boldest, blackest face ever to be released in type. When released, it gave new meaning to the term "heavyweight."

Even its physical dimensions were awesome: a font of 120-point type weighed well over 80 pounds! Cooper said of his creation, "it's for far-sighted printers with near-sighted customers." Conservative typographers hated the design; even Oz himself had a few reservations, but everybody else loved the face. Graphic designers couldn't get enough of it, printers and advertising typographers couldn't order enough sizes, and BB&S couldn't produce enough fonts. Cooper Black soon became the single best-selling type of the Barnhart Brothers & Spindler foundry.

Rival foundries copied the design —some even pirating the Cooper name. American Type Founders tried to counter the popularity of Cooper Black with their own heavyweight under the famous Goudy name, but nothing could catch up with the runaway popularity of Oz Cooper's first friendly fat-face.

Cooper Black was followed in 1924 by the italic companion to Oz's first face, Cooper, or what was then called Cooper Oldstyle. (The management at Barnhart Brothers & Spindler changed its mind, and thus the name "Cooper.") The new companion italic has an almost naive quality and is much more in keeping with Cooper's hand lettering style than the more conservative roman design. Cooper himself said of the design "it is so much closer to its parent pen form than the roman that freedom is almost the life of it, and readers' eyes do not resent in italic, so much as in roman, departure from familiar regularity. I have dared for this reason to give the italic more novelty than I gave the roman."

In 1925, Barnhart Brothers & Spindler released what was, in all likelihood, the easiest face they ever produced. By simply engraving a white line along the edge of characters in Cooper Black, they created Cooper Hilite.

Cooper Black Italic followed Cooper Hilite in 1926 and quickly joined the ranks of BB&S's best-selling typefaces. Like Cooper Oldstyle Italic, Oz had some fun with this face. In this design he added a dozen or so swash letters that he intended for occasional use as alternatives. But they caught the imagination of graphic designers and ended up being used as much as, if not more than, their more traditional counterparts.

## To Kern, or Not to Kern . . .

In this and his other italic designs, Cooper insisted that all the letters be non-kerning; that is, none of the letters were to overhang the main body of the metal type. While putting roadblocks in the path of perfect spacing, this eliminated the major cause of type breakage in the days of handsetting with metal type. Sometimes Oz Cooper's Midwest practicality overruled his sense of esthetics.

Cooper Black Condensed also appeared in 1926. Cooper described this design as "condensed but not squeezed." In addition to being narrower, Cooper Black Condensed is also about 20 percent less heavy than its big brother, and Oz hoped that it would be used in many applications where the Black was just too much type.

Cooper Fullface is arguably the most innovative of Cooper's creations. It was released by Barnhart Brothers & Spindler shortly before the foundry closed in 1929, and production was taken over by the huge conglomerate of American Type Founders. (ATF renamed the style "Cooper Modern.")

In Cooper Modern, Oz had taken on the difficult task of melding the traits of one of typography's most formal designs, Bodoni, with his own somewhat freewheeling lettering style. Of this face Cooper wrote, "it differs from Bodoni in that its serifs are rounded, and its main stems drawn freely, with a suggestion of curve in almost every line." He added that "It is unusual in that it combines the sharp contrast of main and minor lines (as in Bodoni) with the free rendering (as in Caslon) of pen drawn letters." The parentheses are Cooper's, and while it's easy to see Bodoni in Cooper Modern, the business about Caslon is stretching the point considerably.

## Sans a Sans

Cooper Modern sold only moderately well, and there had been plans to add a companion italic to the offering, but none was completed before the ATF takeover of Barnhart Brothers & Spindler. After the takeover, ATF continued to offer the roman design but did not add any additional faces to complement the original.

Cooper never created a sans serif type, but he did much lettering in a sans serif style long before types like Futura and Kabel were released. Some time after sans serifs began to appear as metal type, Cooper wrote, "I myself have long had the sans serif complex. . . . Updike says sans serif letters are only skeletons for letters, and I would like to prove some time that they are better than that."

Under pressure from the BB&S foundry, Cooper also created a series of initial letters that he didn't much care for, and a group of Christmas ornaments that he downright hated.

Finally Oz drew the basis of two faces on which ATF had others do the final work. Boul Mich (named for Chicago's Michigan Boulevard) is a sans of sorts, in the tradition of ATF's more successful design, Broadway. Actually, Boul Mich may even predate Broadway by a month or two.

Dietz Text is a complicated pen-drawn black letter initially drawn by August Dietz. ATF liked the design but found the original renderings unsuitable for development into fonts of type. Cooper was given the task of making the unworkable, workable.

## Reluctant Autobiographer

Yielding to many requests from friends, Oz Cooper once started writing his autobiography. He completed about four paragraphs, then gave up. Fortunately, the page of handwritten notes was saved

PROMOTIONAL LETTERING BY COOPER

A POSTER DESIGNED BY COOPER, 1923

from the wastebasket into which it had been thrown. Later it was put to use as copy in a commemorative book on Cooper and his work. This is how Oz began his autobiography:

"Born in Ohio, brought up in Coffeyville, Kansas, on the border of Indian Territory and on the edge of the Wild West. At fifteen began as a printer's apprentice, during long school vacation (5 months). Returned next summer to same job with enthusiasm. No pay; second summer one dollar a week. (Supplemental reading: Mark Twain on Pay for Apprentices.) Quit school at seventeen, making raspberry noise, having flunked algebra, geometry, history, Latin, physics. Still consider mathematics as subject for mathematicians, same as music for musicians. Returned again to print shop to stay until twenty, when swept into Chicago by urge to become great illustrator."

Well, Oz never became that great illustrator. He did, however, accomplish just about everything else he set his mind to. The list was not complicated:

Make a living in the graphic arts.

Open a typography studio.

Draw letters well.

Somewhere along the line, "marry childhood sweetheart" was probably also added to the list, because that's what Oz did at the age of 41.

The two Coopers lived a quiet life, preferring the simple pleasures of the country (to which they escaped every summer) to the excitement offered by Chicago (the city in which they lived). Mrs. Cooper once wrote, "We never doubted our life seemed pretty drab and uninteresting to the average person, but to us it was one of such complete affection and understanding that there doesn't seem to be much more I can say about it. We were quietly—perhaps selfishly—content."

Oz Cooper began his design career in 1904, when he entered into partnership

SANS SERIF LETTERFORMS DRAWN BY COOPER

with Fred Bertsch. It ended in 1940 when he died of cancer at age 61.

## More Than a Few Faces

Oswald Cooper was a great designer, one of the greatest that American graphic art has known. An esthete, ever abstemious, deeply modest, genuinely self-effacing, he was his own severest critic. Oz rarely took a vacation but was not a slave to his work. He possessed a strong personal style which, though he never suggested others should follow, influenced American graphics for generations. Oz Cooper created trends. The graphic arts community remembers Oz primarily for his super-bold type, but there is more to this man's work—much more.

# William Addison Dwiggins

## 1880–1956

William Addison Dwiggins never intended to be type designer. He wanted to be an illustrator and to design books. He worked hard and excelled at both professions. But Dwiggins could not turn down a design challenge; and that is how it all started.

The challenge came from C. H. Griffith, the person responsible for typographic development at Mergenthaler Linotype in the early part of this century. Griffith first learned of Dwiggins from an article he read in the trade press. The article dealt with the current state of the typographic arts, and in it Dwiggins complained that there were no acceptable gothic typefaces available for Linotype composition. Furthermore, Dwiggins stated, there were no good text gothics designed in America. (Franklin and News Gothic were considered display faces.) Upon seeing Dwiggins' article, Griffith sent him a letter which, in essence, said, "If you think you're so good, let's see the gothic you can draw."

The challenge was accepted, and thus began the 27-year association between Mergenthaler Linotype and William Dwiggins. Seventeen typeface families came out of the partnership. The first, of course, was a gothic—Metro—the now-classic newspaper face. Four additional families were published; the remaining typefaces were experimental. The association of Dwiggins with Mergenthaler established him as one of America's most important typeface designers. It did not, however, divert Dwiggins from pursuing his other loves.

He was a prolific book designer, a gifted calligrapher, a professional illustrator, and graphic designer. He was a talented writer, historian, and teacher. In fact, Dwiggins' book on layout design became a major text on the subject. He also designed and produced furniture—and he even painted murals.

Dwiggins' major source of income was from his book designs. There are over 290 titles to his credit. In fact, many are now collected as works of art.

Dwiggins' artistic endeavors were not limited to those for which he received professional income. The children of Hingham, Massachusetts (where he lived and worked), knew Bill Dwiggins for his marionettes and kites. In the 30-seat marionette theater he designed and built below his studio, Dwiggins was playwright, artist, director, and producer. In

DWIGGINS AT WORK. REPRINTED COURTESY LINOTYPE COMPANY.

addition, he made all the marionettes that performed—even one of himself (should the audience cry "author" at the end of a performance).

In the spring and fall, Dwiggins made kites for the enjoyment of the neighborhood children. And, although he did not invent the device, some say he perfected the kite trolley. This was a mobilelike contraption that could sail up a kite string. When it touched the kite paper, parachutes were released to float to earth, or into the hands of small children.

Dwiggins found fun in all his work. It is obvious in everything he created. While perhaps less apparent in his typeface designs (each is the result of a serious and contemplative study of a particular design challenge), Bill did little that was not enjoyable for him.

Caledonia, Dwiggins' best-known and most popular typeface, was first begun as a revival design. One of the challenges to himself in this design program was to create an updated version of the Scotch type style popular at the end of the nineteenth century. In doing so, he tried to combine the basic Scotch design with other, then popular, text typefaces. Dwiggins tried Scotch mixed with Bodoni, Scotch with Baskerville, and Scotch with Caslon. None of these preliminary designs, however, met with his satisfaction; and after several false starts, he decided to abandon the goal of reviving Scotch. (Scotch doesn't stay Scotch if you sweat the fat off it.) He began to create a more original design, and Caledonia emerged, a typeface loosely based on one used by Bulmer in the late 18th century.

Dwiggins had two goals for the Caledonia design program, however, and the second objective was not changed or modified. That was to create a typeface for a mechanical typesetter, the Linotype, which could be used in books of beauty and clarity. This became the underlying challenge in all his type design work: to create beautiful and effective typefaces for machine composition.

Time has proved that Dwiggins more than met his goals. Even now, more than 45 years after the original release

of Caledonia, it is still one of the most popular text styles. Its beauty and communicative power still prevail. While Dwiggins' first typeface design, Metro, no longer enjoys wide popularity, it remained, until recently, a mainstay of newspaper typography.

It is said that Metro was the only typeface in which Dwiggins let his sense of humor show through. The capitals "A" through "P" have the crisp quality of a mechanical drawing, an apparent geometric precision, but in the "Q" Dwiggins indulged himself; he had fun. The tail of the "Q" seems whimsical—and certainly out of character with the rest of the design.

Eldorado, another Dwiggins typeface, is not one of his better known typestyles—at least not yet. That design program was begun at the urging of several Latin-American publishers. They asked Mergenthaler Linotype to develop a book type that would reflect the flavor of the Spanish typographic tradition. Dwiggins was delighted to take on the project. It was a natural for him, a chance to create a beautiful typeface based on research and study of a particular design problem.

Something else influenced the Eldorado design program: World War II. Begun at the outbreak of the war, the typeface reflects the wartime regulations for the conservation of paper. Dwiggins endeavored to create a face that would provide maximum spatial economy without sacrificing the beauty or readability of the design. Eldorado was completed in 1951 but did not reach popularity—until perhaps now.

Recently Mergenthaler Linotype undertook the revival of Dwiggins' original Eldorado. The design talents of John Quaranta, a man who transferred some of Dwiggins' original work into drawings for type matrices, and the electronic capability of the Ikarus software, were brought together for this project. It is fitting that the craft of letter drawing and electronic technology are combined in this program. Dwiggins always tried to incorporate into his type designs the tra-

YOUNG BILL DWIGGINS. REPRINTED PERMISSIONS FOR THE AIGA DWIGGINS EXHIBITION KEEPSAKE, 1957. PHOTO: MRS. WILLIAM DOYLE.

DWIGGINS. REPRINTED PERMISSIONS FOR THE AIGA DWIGGINS EXHIBITION KEEPSAKE, 1957. PHOTO: ARTHUR GRIFFIN.

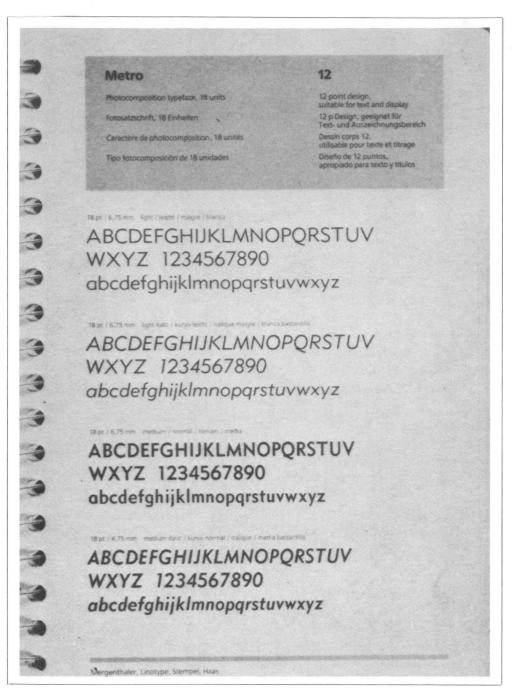

SPECIMEN SHOWING OF METRO. REPRINTED COURTESY LINOTYPE COMPANY.

ditions of the past with the requirements of the present and future. John Quaranta's hand and design skills provided the tradition; he created the basic weights required for this revival program. Ikarus software built on the sign foundation created by Quaranta and produced a full typeface family. The designer and the computer worked together to modify Dwiggins' original design where necessary, to make it compatible with current typographic needs. Only time will tell if this new design will successfully carry on the Dwiggins heritage.

While Dwiggins' typefaces were the result of careful study and diligent effort—serious business—he never took the end result seriously. Probably the most severe, and certainly the most humorous, judgments of his work have been written by Dwiggins himself, in the guise of a Dr. Hermann Puterschein.

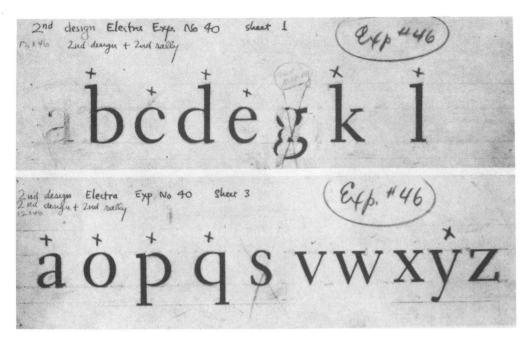

ORIGINAL DRAWING FOR ELECTRA. REPRINTED COURTESY LINOTYPE COMPANY.

He created the sarcastic and sometimes bombastic Doctor early in his career. Dr. Puterschein was supposed to be a transplanted German of irrefutable typographic knowledge and taste. Aside from being the chief critic of Dwiggins' work, Dr. Puterschein was also the only officer of the mythical Society of Calligraphers, a group which Dwiggins created, and inducted into membership such designers as Frederic Goudy, Rudolph Ruzicka and Bruce Rogers. At one point, Dwiggins even started the rumor that he was, in fact, the imaginative personality assumed by Dr. Puterschein.

Like so many other Dwiggins creations, Dr. Puterschein lives on today. A new generation of young type designers, working for a major manufacturer of photocomposition equipment, became great fans of Dwiggins and his work. They were also enchanted by his imaginary personality, Dr. Puterschein, and they adopted the Doctor as their own. Some of these young designers left that original company to work elsewhere in the business—and took the Doctor with them. As a result, Hermann Puterschein will now be copied occasionally on an interoffice memo at Compugraphic Corporation, or paged on the intercom at Itek. He has cropped up at Autologic, AM Varityper, Information International, and Xerox. Every once in a while, a postcard even arrives at ITC, signed "Doctor Hermann Puterschein."

Apart from the fictitious Doctor, few have found fault with Dwiggins' type design efforts. If any criticism can be leveled, it is that he did not produce enough typefaces. Perhaps the criticisms are justified, because Dwiggins is certainly better remembered today for his type designs than for his puppets, his furniture, his illustrations, or his book designs.

William Dwiggins was born in Martinsville, Ohio, in 1880. While little is written about his early life, it can be assumed from his lively wit and humor that his childhood was happy. At age 19 he went to Chicago to study at the Frank Holme School of Illustration. It was there that he met Frederic Goudy. When Goudy moved to the suburbs of Boston and established the Village Press, he invited young Dwiggins to join him to work as a book designer and illustrator. It did not pay much, but Dwiggins was happy; he loved his work and came to love New England.

When Goudy moved to New York, Dwiggins remained in Boston; he

DWIGGINS LATE IN LIFE. REPRINTED
PERMISSIONS FOR THE AIGA
DWIGGINS EXHIBITION KEEPSAKE,
1957. PHOTO: DOROTHY ABBE.

had found his home. Dwiggins built a studio across from his house and continued to work there the rest of his life.

Dwiggins enjoyed his work and liked to work. He is quoted as saying "Like to design type. Like to jiggle, type around and see what comes out. Like to design ornament. Like paper. Like ink on paper. Like bright colors. Handicapped by clock." On Christmas morning, 1956, the clock ran out. The life of a man who contributed much to the esthetic values of the printing world came to an end.

The design community mourned Dwiggins' death as the passing of a friend, more than of a co-worker. The Dwiggins household was deluged with flowers and letters of sympathy.

There were a few, however, who possibly sighed with relief at Dwiggins' departure. His many, and diverse, interests often detracted from his ability to maintain the design schedules for typeface development. This presented problems. Mergenthaler Linotype's files record instances of missed deadlines and extended work schedules. On one occasion, when Dwiggins was acting for Mergenthaler as a design consultant on other designers' efforts, his procrastination during an important review cycle held up the design process of a particular typeface for a very long time. The artist's efforts were delayed to the point that he began to make anonymous threatening phone calls to C. H. Griffith and his boss, the president of Mergenthaler. Fortunately, the threats were not carried out and Dwiggins did

ultimately finish the typeface review. In fact, that typeface is still, more than 30 years later, one of Mergenthaler's more popular typeface designs.

The end result of any design project Dwiggins worked on was always of lasting beauty, supreme functionalism, and extraordinary zeal. Another of Dwiggins' imaginary personalities, Kobodaishi (a patron saint of the lettering art and a great Buddhist missionary in ancient Japan) perhaps best summed up the work of this master of design. Kobodaishi's words were in reference to Caledonia, but they hold true for all Dwiggins' work: "Electricity, sparks, energy . . . positive —say it with a snap . . . Make a line of letters so full of energy that it can't wait to get to the end of the measure."

In addition to creating beauty with letterforms, Dwiggins did something else: He accepted, and met, the challenge of developing esthetically pleasing typefaces for a new and supposedly inferior output medium—the Linotype. The longevity of his design testifies to his success at meeting the challenge.

Thankfully, there are more designers like Dwiggins. It is the designers who followed in his footsteps who gave us our classic typefaces for machine composition, the phototype faces we currently use, and soon the typefaces we will be using on electronic and impact printing devices. Dwiggins can serve as a model to any designer who is called on to create beauty in spite of challenging odds.

# Eric Gill

## 1882–1947

A former apprentice once wrote to Eric Gill about a moral perplexity. It concerned whether or not to carve a memorial to the Fascist dead in the Spanish Civil War, a monument that would be exhibited in London to raise funds for Franco's cause. Gill was a lifelong opponent of Fascism, and at the time was a member of an international artist's society against oppression. Gill replied to the former apprentice by postcard: "Plenty biz no do! No biz do!"

Seemingly contradictory advice from a staunch and active supporter of human rights. And yet, Gill was a man of many contradictions. He was a fervent convert to Catholicism; at the same time he was able to maintain equally ardent, and exceptionally liberal, views on sexual relationships. A friend once said that when Gill became a Catholic, he thought of everything in terms of religion, including sex; and that later he thought of everything in terms of sex, including religion.

Gill loved train engines all his life, but he insisted that as far as he could, he would avoid the use of all machines and their products. No cars, no phones, and no radios were permitted on the grounds of his studio.

Gill lived always on the edge of poverty, but this was by choice. It was consistent with his need for asceticism and his contempt for the products of industrial society. He never charged much for his work; most of the time only the stonemason's daily wage of about £2. He would, however, insist upon traveling by train—first class—when it was at the expense of his patrons.

BRUSH-DRAWN CALLIGRAPHY, EARLY 1920S. REPRINTED WITH
PERMISSION FROM *THE LETTER FORMS AND TYPE DESIGNS OF ERIC GILL* BY
ROBERT HARLING. LONDON: HURTWOOD PRESS, 1976.

## SMALL BUT IMPORTANT CONTRIBUTIONS

When compared to the work of Benton, Goudy, or Benguiat, the quality of Eric Gill's typeface designs might appear slight. His contributions to typography would seem thin were it not for the importance and beauty of the typefaces he created. His two best-known designs, Gill Sans and Perpetua, are internationally regarded among the most beautiful, readable, and intellectually well-conceived typefaces of modern times. A couple of his lesser-known designs, Felicity and Joanna Italic, have been called two of the most graceful types available to 20th-century typographers. Gill brought to handset and machine composition the beauty and grace of calligraphic and inscripted letterforms. His contribution was one of quality rather than quantity.

Gill made the typographic communicator's palette richer, but he had few kind words for the art of typography. At different times he is quoted as saying, "there are now about as many different varieties of letters as there are fools," "lettering has had its day," and "the only way to reform modern lettering is to abolish it." Once he referred to master printers as "a bunch of morons."

The second of 13 children, Eric Gill was born February 3, 1882, in Brighton, England. His father was a clergyman and his mother had been a professional singer.

Gill began to draw at an early age. This fondness for rendering and his love of railway engines are probably what led Gill to letterforms, and eventually to typography. "If you are keen on engines," he once wrote, "you collect engine names . . . and if you draw engines you cannot leave out their names." (In those years, train engines had their names in large letters along the boiler.)

At 17, Gill got his first job, in a London architect's office. But more important, he also attended Edward Johnston's first lettering class. The impact of Johnston's teaching on young Gill was immediate, profound, and lasting: "He . . . altered the whole course of my life and all my ways of thinking." They were to become the closest of friends and even shared housing until Johnston's marriage.

## COMMUNAL LIVING

At 25, Gill moved from London to a more pastoral environment in Ditchling, England, one more in keeping with his philosophical attitudes. Over the next several months Ditchling was to evolve into the first of three communal localities in which Gill lived and was the moving force. Those who gathered around Gill and his family at Ditchling, then Capel-y-ffin, and finally Pigotts were similarly motivated to seek artistic independence and simple self-sufficiency. But above all, they were united by their religious convictions. All were devout, if somewhat unorthodox, Catholics. Several of the men in the communities even went on to become Tertiaries in the order of St. Dominic.

Gill had three children, all daughters, and all born within a very short span of time. Probably he would have had several more children (being Catholic, from a large family himself, and predisposed toward an active sexual life). His wife, Elizabeth, however, had suffered complications from a miscarried fourth child and was unable to continue bearing children.

Gill was a man of order. He managed his life and his work through a strict system of self-imposed rules and regulations. It has been said that his steadfast reliance on those rules might have stifled his creativity and ultimately weakened his artistic output.

## THE UNHOLY CATHOLIC

One area, however, in which Gill consistently failed to follow the rules he professed to believe in (those of the Catholic

BOOKPLATE, 1909. REPRINTED WITH PERMISSION FROM *THE LETTER FORMS AND TYPE DESIGNS OF ERIC GILL* BY ROBERT HARLING. LONDON: HURTWOOD PRESS, 1976.

TRAIN DRAWING BY YOUNG GILL. REPRINTED WITH PERMISSION FROM *THE LETTER FORMS AND TYPE DESIGNS OF ERIC GILL* BY ROBERT HARLING. LONDON: HURTWOOD PRESS, 1976.

CHRISTMAS CARD, 1908. REPRINTED WITH PERMISSION FROM *THE LETTER FORMS AND TYPE DESIGNS OF ERIC GILL* BY ROBERT HARLING. LONDON: HURTWOOD PRESS, 1976.

ABCDEFGHIJKLMNO
PQRSTUVWXYZ
abcdefghijklmnopqrst
uvwxyz

ABCDEFGHIJKLMN
OPQRSTUVWXYZ
abcdefghijklmnopqrs
tuvwxyz

THIS is a specimen of the *Aries* type designed by Eric Gill in 18 point, 14 point and 10 point roman and *italic* for Fairfax Hall at The Stourton Press. (*That was 18 point. This is 14 point italic, followed by a sentence in roman and the final sentence is in 10 point.*)

This is a specimen of 36-point Joanna in the Monotype version Series 478 and this is *Joanna Italic*.

Church), and where his rationality and will power were consistently set aside, was in his sexual life. His many diaries, autobiography, and countless other writings document this area in explicit detail. His private drawings and sculpture also reflect this predilection. There was, however, never any perversity in his attitude toward sex. In fact, there was an almost innocent naiveté displayed. He said it was "not so much sensuality as curiosity, the desire to know rather than to feel," which drove his compulsion. A critic commenting on Gill's erotic works once said that England has always lacked an artist able to celebrate all the moods of love—from the sublime to the ridiculous—and that perhaps if the best of his private drawings were more widely known, Gill might emerge as a leading contender for the title.

After 17 years, Gill moved from Ditchling to Capel-y-ffin in Wales. The single word to describe Capel-y-ffin is "remote." It was 10 miles to the nearest railroad station, 15 miles from a village of any size, and was accessible only by foot or pony cart.

A visitor described the weather at Capel-y-ffin as raining continuously, ". . . the house was damp—the paper in my bedroom leaned crazily away from all four walls—there was no hot water, no newspapers, spartan food—and I enjoyed every instant of my visit: Gill's sharp-edged and genial talk warmed the bleak house." Apparently, those who lived there all the time were not quite so impressed. After taking as much as they could tolerate, the women at one point rebelled and moved to a more comfortable setting at Pigotts near High Wycombe. Gill and the other men soon followed.

He lived at Pigotts until his premature death from lung cancer in 1940. His wife, who, despite his many lapses into sexual adventure, was the lifelong focus of his deepest love, survived Gill at Pigotts until 1961.

## ANOTHER LATE BLOOMER

As familiar as the name Gill is to typo-philes, he did not create his first typeface until well past 40. To many, Eric Gill is better known as a sculptor, a profession he worked at before, during, and after his efforts as a typeface designer. His work in this area can be seen in the United Kingdom and throughout the world. His sculpture is over the doors of the BBC offices in Portland Place; the Stations of the Cross in Westminster Cathedral are Gill's work; a statue of his holds a place of honor in the sculpture garden at UCLA in Los Angeles; and a massive carved re-lief, which was a gift of England to the League of Nations building in Geneva, is also Gill's.

From his very early years, Gill re-belled against the industrialization of the late 19th and early 20th centuries. He was especially influenced by the teachings of the Fabian Society, which was strong in England at the time.

Gill vowed that he would not en-gage in the "malevolent" practices of in-dustry. While Gill knew he was a talented artist and designer with potential, he also knew that he had little likelihood of build-ing a successful business while following such unconventional theories.

ABCDEFGHIJKLMNO
abcdefghijklmnopqrstuv
ABDEGHJKMNQRS
abcdefghijklmnopqrs

STRUCTURAL SIMILARITIES BETWEEN PERPETUA AND GILL SANS.

ABCDEFGH
IKLMNOPR
STUWXYabcde
fghijklmnopqrstuwxy

Deliberately, therefore, Gill set about learning a trade that would provide him with some degree of steady income, allow him to work with a certain amount of freedom at his artistic endeavors, and not conflict with his philosophy of life. This didn't leave much room for choice. Masonry and lettercutting, however, soon became a natural and logical path. Through the teachings and guidance of Johnston, Gill became an accomplished calligrapher and lettering artist. These skills and his training as a stonemason lead him, by degrees, to the profession of stone carving. At first his commissions were few; but as his skills developed, so did the demand for his work.

As a result, by 1906 Gill had to employ his first assistant, a lad of 15. Over the next 34 years, Gill had 26 more assistants or apprentices who worked for and studied under him.

Because of his social and philosophical views, there can be little doubt that Gill saw type designs as working for the enemy. Yet before his life was over,

Gill Sans Cameo, *Monotype Series 233*

Gill Sans Shadow Line, *Monotype Series 290*

Gill Sans Cameo Ruled, *Monotype Series 299*

Gill Sans Shadow, *Monotype Series 304*

Gill Sans Shadow, *Monotype Series 406*

Gill Sans Ultra Bold, *Monotype Series 442*

A FEW OF THE GILL SANS DERIVATIVES

he created 11 typefaces, wrote an influential book on typography, and operated (with his son-in-law) a commercial press.

## SIMILAR CONVERTS

The major contributing factor in Gill's conversion to typography was Stanley Morison. (There are also those who allude to the friendly "nagging" of Beatrice Warde.) Perhaps it was because Morison was so much like Gill that he was able to exert such an influence. Morison, too, was a self-taught, self-made man. He also had a similar reputation for dogmatism and perfection. And, like Gill, he was a converted Catholic.

Morison saw his task as typographical advisor to the Monotype Corporation to change the "stiff, thin, regimental and savorless," typefaces then in use for designs that better reflected current typographic technology, thinking, and attitudes. After reviving several classical faces such as Bembo, Fournier, and Poliphilus, he felt that a truly modern face, designed by a living artist, should be released; and Morison thought Gill ideal for the task.

Morison felt that a serif typeface would be the best, most logical choice for such a design. He also believed that the serif was "not in origin calligraphic but epigraphic; not written but sculpted. It follows then that the drawings for this new type could be best made by a sculptor or stonecutter." Gill was both, and thus the natural choice. Retention of the chiseled quality of Gill's letterforms became of primary importance to Morison.

In 1925, Gill began his initial studies for the typeface that was to become Perpetua. Experiments, trial cuttings, and many revisions of the typeface went on for several years, delaying the release. It was during this time that Morison also persuaded Gill to work on a new sans serif style.

Although the work was entirely his, there were two strong influences on the "sans" Gill developed. The strongest was the work that his mentor, Johnston, did for the London Underground Railroad. This was a sans serif they commissioned for their publicity department, a design program on which Gill consulted with Johnston in the early stages. The end result was a beautiful and simple "sans" with obvious design traits that are echoed in Gill's work. The other influence was a set of alphabets Gill created for the British Army and Navy stores. Both influences were, however, typefaces created primarily for signage purposes, and they do differ in important, if subtle, ways from the "sans" Gill did for the Monotype Corporation.

## DIFFICULT BEGINNINGS

When first shown at a trade conference in 1928, Gill Sans was greeted with disapproval and cries of "typographical bolshevism." A year later, when it was released to the public, the cries had subsided. The face soon became the most popular "sans" used in Britain and the United Kingdom. It was not until after World War II that Gill Sans was exported to the United States.

Gill's original sans serif spawned some 36 derivatives, not all designed by Gill. In fact, some he rejected outright. Sans stands, however, as Gill's most pronounced achievement in the field of typeface design. The face is somewhat unusual in that the letterforms are patterned after roman character shapes and proportions rather than those found in more common sans serif designs. As a result, Gill Sans has often been called the most readable and legible sans serif design.

The first showing of Gill's roman was in a private printing of a translation of *The Passion of Perpetua and Felicity*, published in 1928. The roman face was thus named Perpetua and the italic, drawn later, Felicity.

The italic was the first major text face to introduce the obliqued roman form as an italic design. This was drawn primarily at the urging of Morison, who

EARLY SANS SERIF SKETCHES. REPRINTED WITH PERMISSION FROM *THE LETTER FORMS AND TYPE DESIGNS OF ERIC GILL* BY ROBERT HARLING. LONDON: HURTWOOD PRESS, 1976.

BOOKPLATE 1920. REPRINTED WITH PERMISSION FROM *THE LETTER FORMS AND TYPE DESIGNS OF ERIC GILL* BY ROBERT HARLING. LONDON: HURTWOOD PRESS, 1976.

believed this style provided improved harmony between the roman and italic in mixed composition. The original italic, as created by Gill, is not, however, the one used with Perpetua today. It was replaced by another obliqued roman simply called Perpetua Italic. It is unfortunate because many feel the more recent italic lacks much of the grace and harmony of Felicity. Even with the new italic, the Perpetua family still retains the strong, incised characteristics sought by Morison.

This cannot be said of Joanna, however, a typeface drawn in 1930 for limited editions work. This family also had the obliqued roman style of italic, but showed a freer, more calligraphic, form than Perpetua. Originally cast for hand composition in just two sizes, the typeface was not made available for public use until 1958. Although recently revived in the United Kingdom for display purposes, Joanna did not achieve the transition into photo and digital text composition.

Gill created an Egyptian (or square serif) design in 1929, called Solus; but this typeface is rare. Perhaps it was never widely accepted because it is practically indistinguishable from Perpetua in text sizes.

If there is a common complaint about Gill's work, it is that he created only one typeface, Perpetua, and several too-subtle derivations. Even Gill Sans has a strong family resemblance to Perpetua.

Jubilee was a calligraphically inspired design originally created as an advertising face for the Cunard Shipping Line. Jubilee is also not available as photo or digital type.

Bunyan is another Gill typeface. It first appeared in 1934 as a release for private press work. In 1953, the face reappeared as Pilgrim, from London Linotype Company, with an italic that was neither available with the original—nor designed by Gill. Several feel that the roman of Bunyan was one of Gill's most successful design efforts.

## THE BASIC, MOST VALUABLE, GOALS

Eric Gill lived a life of continual activity. He was a writer, printer, painter, illustrator, sculptor, calligrapher, stone cutter, and type designer. He was often argumentative and contradictory. At times he was misguided in his approach to typography. His basic goals, however, were important, consistent, and worth emulating. They were to create, "Absolutely legible-to-the-last-degree letters, provide beauty of form to all printed communication, and to maintain the dignity of hand drawn letterforms." Here there were no contradictions.

## Stanley Morison

### 1889–1967

Stanley Morison belonged to a number of British "men's clubs." By current standards they would be considered old-fashioned, stuffy, and probably elitist. A story is told that when a member of one of the clubs married a young waitress who worked there, the staff and most of the other members were surprised and astonished. But not Morison. He had been the couple's confidant and one of the major influences in their decision.

A photograph of Stanley Morison would appear to reveal a somber, aloof gentleman, a man confident with his power and above the petty aspects of day-to-day life. Photographs can be deceiving. While the power and strength are real, what is not seen in the photograph is Morison's gift for friendship, his unerring and passionate sense of morality and devotion to his faith. Neither does it show Morison's need for anonymity. To him, the cause, the institution, was always greater than those who took part.

The waitress story is typical. Morison was a great friend, advisor, and motivator to the couple, yet no one knew. He was devoted to many causes, a diligent and influential force in each, but he almost always chose to remain in the background.

His interests and achievements were many and varied, yet because of Morison's need for anonymity, few are well known. On the surface he was outgoing, open, and a "joiner," but this was just a facade. Surrounded by acquaintances, a man of many friendships, Morison was lonely still. He knew many people; few knew him. He cared deeply for others and frequently became involved with their lives, yet few could penetrate the false front he presented to the world.

## BASIC BLACK

Morison always wore black: black coat, black pants, black shoes, black socks, black tie, black hat, even a black watch fob. His only variance from black cloth-ing was his white shirt. He appeared to be the personification of British social and political conservatism, but nothing could be further from the truth. A man of great love and dedication to his country, Morison was, nonetheless, completely opposed to British (or any other form of) monarchy and nobility. In his youth, Morison was a pacifist. In 1914, he refused to fight when Britain went to war —and as a result spent two years in prison. He was also a Marxist and close friend to most of the original members of the British Communist Party.

Once, offered a knighthood as a reward for designing stamps for the Postal Service, Morison, true to form, promptly refused. Morison would have neither the notoriety nor the title.

Morison was what many would consider the most passionate kind of Catholic—a convert. His love of the Church and one of its most traditional forms of music, the Gregorian chant, remained with him throughout his life.

The deep feelings and dedication were not confined to heavy philosophical and moral issues. Morison was an avid stamp collector. Like Eric Gill, he loved trains. He was a lifelong cricket fan; and, it is said, he was never happier than when having champagne at lunch.

## CONFLICTING PASSIONS

Not always in neat little boxes, sometimes Morison's passions conflicted. On a number of occasions he tried to join the British Communist Party, but the members felt that his mixture of orthodox Marxism and devout Catholicism was an unsuitable basis for party membership. When he was in his mid-thirties, Morison met Beatrice Warde, and soon his admiration and respect for this young woman's talent and ability turned into something much deeper. Married, and a faithful Catholic, his passions once again caused conflicts.

Intensely rational and skeptical yet possessing complete religious faith, jovial

THE *TIMES* OF LONDON BEFORE AND AFTER MORISON REDESIGNED THE PAPER. THE OCTOBER 3, 1932 ISSUE WAS ONE OF THE FIRST TO FEATURE TIMES NEW ROMAN.

yet ascetic, a convinced Marxist yet a close friend of capitalists and nobility, Morison was a man of many paradoxes. Though his passions were varied and intense, it is Stanley Morison's love and dedication to the typographic arts that compel us to remember him. It has been said that Morison found typography without organized history or principles, and left it with both. He became probably this century's most influential authority on printing and the typographic arts. Responsible for the design of some of the most outstanding typefaces produced in the last hundred years, he became one of the first publication design consultants when he redesigned *The Times* of London.

Few people can identify any single event that changed the path of their career growth. Even fewer can identify the exact date of that event. Stanley Morison was unconventional in this area also. It was on September 10, 1912, that he changed from an undirected youth wandering through life and career, to become driven and aimed.

There was nothing to distinguish this day from any other. Morison was, he said, on the way home from his job as a bank teller when his eye caught a glimpse of the Printing Supplement published by *The Times* newspaper that day. He recalled that the cover was striking and easily distinguished from other periodicals and journals on the bookstall. Morison purchased the supplement, and his life was changed.

The publication contained articles on the history of printing, current trends in advertising, the work of important individuals, the current state of the printing arts, and typesetting systems. After the articles there were beautiful advertisements for printing services, booksellers, and typefaces. One publication provided a beautiful, intelligent, and powerful overview of the craft of printing and typesetting. Morison was overwhelmed, and instantly "hooked" on type.

One of the advertisements in the supplement was for a new magazine to be dedicated to the typographic arts. The ad presented the publication's goals and an-

GILL SANS 262
ABDEGHKMN
abcdefghjkmop
*abcdefghjkmopq*

GILL SANS

nounced its founders. Though production of the magazine was several months off, Morison knew that he somehow had to be associated with the periodical and its publishers.

## The First Issue and the First Career Step

He must have been one of the first to purchase *The Imprint* when it was first published in January of the following year. Not only did the text and illustrations surpass Morison's expectations, but a short paragraph at the end of the editorial "Notes" ran as follows:

*Note: We require at the offices of* The Imprint *the services of a young man of good education and preferably some experience in publishing and advertising. We prefer that applications should, in the first, be made by letter, addressed to the Business Editor,* The Imprint, *11 Henrietta Street, Covent Garden, London.*

Morison had none of the qualifications, but his desire to work on such a potentially important journal, and with such eminent professionals, overcame normal judgment. He applied for the job, and soon, to his excitement and astonishment, found himself hired. But, *The Imprint,* like the candle that burns too brightly, quickly burned itself out. Morison went on to other jobs—always within the printing industry.

In the years that followed, Morison became an accomplished typographer and designer; his reputation and circle of acquaintances grew. He began to hold informal meetings in his office after normal work hours for those interested in fine printing. At one of these gatherings he and four others decided to form a publishing society that, among other things, would produce a journal each year to demonstrate that composing machines could produce typography as beautiful as handset type in private presses. It was to be called The Fleuron Society.

Unfortunately, the society was never to be (the founders were ultimately unable to settle on its goals), but the idea of publishing a fine print journal, and the name *Fleuron,* were carried on by Morison and another great British typographer, Oliver Simon. *The Fleuron* was eventually printed and appeared six times between 1923 and 1930. The first four issues were edited by Oliver Simon and the last three by Morison; but Morison was to a large extent the editor from the beginning. *The Fleuron* was intended to be an educational tool. It was Morison's plan to "improve the quality of printing, not by improving the printer, but by improving that much more important man, the printer's customer." Each volume was handsome, some even say lavish, and something unusual for such a remarkable publication—very low priced. The mid-20th century, however, was not much different from current conditions, in that handsome and grand publications cannot be produced inexpensively. Since low purchase price was very important to Morison, he consequently lost money on each issue. Many years were spent repaying the debts he incurred while producing *The Fleuron.*

*The Fleuron* contained articles on typeface design and the work of various designers and typographers. The articles were penetrating, incisive, and often critical. In those days, Morison was referred to by some of the die-hards in printing as a "typographical Bolshevik." In spite of (or perhaps because of) this, *The Fleuron* won recognition and quickly became influential—not only in England but in the United States, Germany, France, and several other countries.

The end of *The Fleuron* was, in a sense, the end of the first decade of Morison's life work. Finishing it, like editing it, was something that grew out of its content. Its end came partly because Morison had run out of ideas and partly because he felt that the pressure of publication was hindering his work in other, more important areas. So, amid the protests of its readers, Morison concluded the last issue with an engraving by Eric Gill of a hand closing Fleuron 7 firmly, with the word EXPLICIT hand lettered above the illustration.

## MAJOR APPOINTMENTS

In the 1920s, Morison was appointed typographical advisor to three institutions: in 1922 to the Monotype Corporation in London; in 1925 to the Cambridge University Press; and in 1929 to *The Times*. The appointments were to continue for over 30 years and it was through them that Morison did most of the work for which he is remembered.

His connection with Monotype and with Cambridge was particularly fortunate for the graphic communications industry. Under Morison's guidance and inspiration, Monotype undertook a program of typeface development that was to be the most aggressive ever attempted in Britain or Europe to that time. Many years later, Morison himself, wrote, ". . . when a plan was laid before the managing director. It was intended as a programme of typographical design, rational, systematic, and corresponding effectively with the foreseeable needs of printing; and it involved the expenditure of a good deal of money and the acceptance of risks that had never been undertaken by a type composing-machine company." Both original typefaces and revivals of old designs were included in the program. Faces such as Centaur, Gill, Perpetua, Ehrhardt Romulus, and Monotype's versions of Bembo, Baskerville, Garamond, Bell and Fournier were released—and, of course, Times New Roman. Each of these, and more than 30 more families, were developed in close connection with the Cambridge University Press, which provided continual and active feedback on how well the typefaces performed under actual use.

Morison first came into regular contact with Monotype in the early months of 1922. They had recently begun to have each issue of the *Monotype Recorder* (a journal which Monotype pub-

lished to entertain and inform its customers) designed and printed by a different printing house which used their equipment. The issue for January/February, 1922, was to be produced and printed at the Cloister Press where Morison was then working. He undoubtedly had a hand in laying out the journal and, in addition, contributed two articles for it.

As a result, Monotype was able to observe, firsthand, Morison's abilities as a typographer, type historian, and authority on type design. They also got a glimpse of his ability to be opinionated and outspoken. In one of the articles, he critiqued the typeface Cheltenham in what has been described as a "splendid diatribe."

## ADVISOR BUT NOT DIPLOMAT

"Splendid" or not, Stanley Morison always spoke with candor—sometimes painfully so. A story is told that when he appeared at an interview for the position of typographical advisor to the Cambridge University Press, the chairman of the Press said, by way of opening the interview, "I understand that you would like to join us." "Only if you are interested in good printing," was Morison's immediate reply.

As Typographical Advisor to Monotype, he provided the corporation with a breathtaking design program. His adaptations of earlier typefaces were designed to bring out the qualities in the original designs best suited to the demands of current technology and standards of typographic usage. In these, and in the original designs he championed, Morison tried to emphasize the best and most efficient communication qualities of each design without blemishing it with too much personality or style.

He believed that the product the type designer developed—the typeface—was infinitely more important than the personal or artistic expression of the designer. His primary complaint with the typographic industry was directed toward

PERPETUA

TIMES NEW ROMAN

type designers who insisted upon putting their "thumbprint" on any face they designed. Morison's comments about Frederic Goudy are typical: "I entertain very decided opinions about this latest of Mr. Goudy's achievements. I don't know why Mr. Goudy allows it (I know he has been ill and perhaps that accounts for it). But it appears to me that his press agent is disgracefully handling the ordinary proprieties of life when he gives Goudy's name the prominence he does. I very much detest the idea that this type was designed by Goudy . . . this sort of typographical nomenclature will only further confuse our present miserably anarchic terminology."

On another occasion, this time in slightly kinder words, he expressed his opinion again, "Beauty is desirable—and beauty will come if unsought. There is nothing so disastrous to typography as beauty for the sake of beauty or change for the sake of change. Mannerisms designed to reflect current philosophical tendencies are only tolerable where they are appropriate—as the waving of a signal. Such novelty as is required by reasonable exercise of the appetite for individuality should be reserved to pages whose decipherment is optional."

## TYPEFACES OF HONEST BEAUTY

The typefaces which Monotype released under Morison's guidance are reflections of that philosophy. They are all beautiful, but the beauty is not forced. For the most part, they are exceptionally versatile typefaces, many of which have stood the test of time to become typographic classics. Most are revivals of previously existing type styles, but a few—notably Gill Sans, Perpetua, and Times New Roman, are new and original designs. A diverse range of typeface designs are the result of the design program and Morison's genius. Exquisite titling faces such as Albertus; sturdy, square serif designs like Rockwell; sans serifs from Eric Gill and Sol Hess; revivals such as Bembo, Basker-

ville, Veronese and Walbaum, are just a part of Morison's typographic contribution.

## JUST LIKE IN THE MOVIES

In 1924, Morison made the first of many visits to America. He wasn't looking forward to the trip. (He didn't think that he would like America much; but he had developed several "postal friendships" with Americans influential in the graphic arts, and the United States was fast becoming an important typographic center.) After much encouragement and prodding by those acquaintances and business associates on both sides of the Atlantic, Morison set sail for America. While in the United States, he met his postal friends; traveled to Boston, Princeton, and New York; and like many first-time travelers to America he came away exhausted. Except for one or two high points, for the most part he felt that his four-week stay had been a waste of time.

Morison didn't know it then, but one incident during this trip (a seemingly insignificant meeting) would change his life. The young assistant librarian at American Type Founders Company's type library had heard about Morison prior to his visit. When she learned from Henry Bullen, her manager and head librarian, that Morison was thinking of traveling to the United States, she wrote to him with an invitation to stay at her, and her husband's, home. Morison declined, but Beatrice Warde, perhaps prompted by curiosity about the stranger so important to British typography, traveled to Boston where Morison was visiting Daniel Updike. She arrived to be greeted by a shout of laughter as Updike was telling his visitor a joke. "I knew," she said, "that the stranger must be Morison." Later she wrote, "He looked like a Jesuit. And when he turned to see who was coming into the room, his momentary frown of curiosity brought his heavy black eyebrows together with formidable effect. What I was not prepared for was the way in which that austere face, somber in repose, could be instantly transfigured by a most captivating schoolboy grin that took at least ten years off his apparent age. . . . Within five minutes of the general conversation that followed I knew that I was in the presence not only of a wit and a scholar, but of a personality more vivid and stimulating than that of anyone I'd ever before encountered."

Beatrice was a beautiful woman, with a strong, almost masculine, profile (later when she was in Britain, Eric Gill used her as the model for a number of his drawings). Morison quickly became aware of her energy, love of type, and eagerness to learn.

In January 1925, Morison succeeded in bringing Beatrice and her husband (an accomplished designer and typographer) to Europe. Her husband was to work on a number of projects for Morison and his acquaintants in the British printing industry. Beatrice went to work as a research assistant to Morison and for the Monotype Corporation. The three worked on a variety of projects.

Slowly the inevitable began to take place. At first, the parties tried to pretend that all was well, (everyone except Morison's wife, who wrote, "A woman stole his real personality . . . a changed man returned (from America)—rough, cruel, indifferent"). Even when the apparent became quite obvious, the three refused to recognize it openly—at least for a while.

In the late summer of 1926, there was an emotional explosion in which everyone was injured. Morison severed all relations with his wife, but being a devout Catholic could not (would not) remarry. He took refuge in work. Beatrice dutifully followed her husband on a business trip which he arranged to separate them from Morison. At this point, however, there was no way to mend the old relationships. Beatrice left her husband, returned to London—and eventually to Stanley Morison. The partnership of Stanley Morison and Beatrice Warde was to endure until his death.

## ANOTHER UNEASY BEGINNING

Morison's association with *The Times* began like that with the Cambridge University Press: on a less-than-ideal note. At the time, he was working with Monotype and was approached by the newspaper to advertise Monotype's type library in a new Printing Supplement (similar to the one that first attracted Morison's interest in 1912). As encouragement, *The Times* offered to set the text copy of the ad at no expense. At this, Morison hit the table with his fist and said vehemently: "We'd do much better to pay them a thousand to keep their comps off it!"

*The Times,* in spite of this less-than-friendly first encounter, was intrigued by Morison's opinion of their grahics, rather than put off by his manner. As a result, several meetings followed to explore the issue. Apparently none went very smoothly; on a number of occasions Morison repeated his opinions on the appearance of the newspaper with such rancor that many of those present were more alarmed by his manner than impressed with his ability. The process of Morison's formal involvement with *The Times* was gradual.

In 1929, he was finally appointed typographic advisor to *The Times*. His immediate task was to redesign the paper —from front page to last. First he tackled the advertising section, replacing almost entirely *The Times* type library in the process. Next came the Printing Supplement itself. Morison not only redesigned the publication, he also contributed a piece on "Newspaper Types."

Next came the type used to set the paper. Several existing type styles were tried first; but Morison and *The Times* executive staff found them unsuitable for one reason or another. These were not arbitrary decisions. *The Times* had a long tradition of providing the news to Londoners, in not only exceptional journalistic styles, but also in what they, at least, believed was exemplary typographic style. Since no existing typeface would do, Morison and *The Times* executive

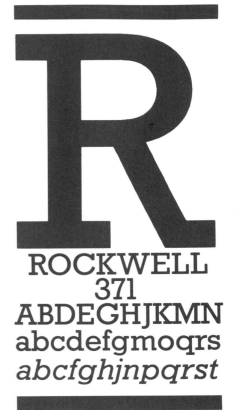

ROCKWELL

staff decided to establish criteria for creating a totally new design. They were basically simple:

- The new design would have to appear larger than its predecessor.
- It could take up no more space than the existing typeface.
- It should be heavier than the existing design.
- It must be highly legible.
- It must be beautiful.

Morison felt that basing the new design on Plantin would begin to satisfy many of the established criteria. Plantin, being a Dutch oldstyle typeface, already has an ample x-height, is somewhat condensed, and its "color" is slightly heavier than normal. Many subtle, and a few not-so-subtle, changes were required, but Plantin's design foundation certainly fulfilled many of the basic requirements.

Victor Lardent, an artist working in *The Times* art department, was assigned the job of typeface design. Morison provided him with photocopies of Plantin specimens and a list of instructions. Thus, the design program was begun, with Morison acting as "creative director" and Lardent as "illustrator/designer." The completed typeface, which was arrived at after a lengthy design process and many revisions, certainly bears a resemblance to Plantin but is also obviously its own design. Serifs had been sharpened from Plantin's, stroke width contrast was increased, and character curves were refined. As a result, Times New Roman is considered a more graceful and elegant design than Plantin.

Times New Roman was first used to print *The Times* in October 1932. One year later, Linotype and Monotype were allowed to offer the family to the typographic community. As released by Monotype Corporation, the face is known as Times New Roman. Linotype calls it simply Times Roman, and *The Times* refers to the face as The Times New Roman.

Over the next 20 years, the typeface was to slowly gain the stature it currently enjoys. It is versatile, legible—and an excellent communicator. And, even more—something often overlooked about this design—it is also beautiful.

In addition to his responsibilities to Monotype, Cambridge University Press, and *The Times,* Stanley Morison was also a talented and prolific writer. He produced a number of substantial works: the four-volume *History of The Times,* the *History of the English Newspaper,* and *The Portraiture of Thomas More.* He also produced a staggering number of articles and essays which he called his "sawdust." They ranged across such diverse topics as the history of Blackletter, English Prayer books, American penmanship—and typography.

## "HE LIVED HIS LIVES"

On October 11, 1967, Morison died. The next day was the scheduled opening of an exhibition on the Fell types of the Cambridge University Press, and the subsequent publication of Morison's book on the same subject. Francis Meynell, the British graphic designer, publisher, and poet, was to deliver the keynote address; instead he improvised an elegy to his friend of 55 years. "This exhibition and this book are a monument to Bishop Fell: they become no less a monument to Stanley Morison. I will not, I could not, speak doleful words about him. He has lived his life. I must amend that conventional phrase—he has lived his lives. We must rejoice in him and his multitudinous works. We must be happily grateful for his devotion—his effective and affectionate devotion—to that combination of historical research and current practice which has been achieved by no one else, in any time, in any country."

# Jan Van Krimpen

## 1892–1958

Jan Van Krimpen wrote virtually volumes on the virtues of cutting type by hand. He extolled as the highest form of type development that which is designed and has punches cut by the same person, and countless times stated that it was the punch cutter's job to take a rough alphabet design and turn it into a usable font of type.

And Van Krimpen worked closely with the same punch cutter on every typeface he drew for the Enschedé type foundry. But in all his voluminous writing, Van Krimpen only once gave credit to his punch cutter and never mentioned his name in print.

Although Van Krimpen is remembered by some as a delightful host and companion, and for the most part extremely generous with his time, there were also occasions when he became suspicious, vain, and obstinate. He refused to discuss certain matters with even his closest friends, and his writings generally lacked the clarity of his graphic work.

Jan Van Krimpen is a man of anomalies—some not very likable.

While not everyone is in agreement about his personal strengths, nearly everyone is in accord regarding Van Krimpen's ability as a typographer; and even some of his staunchest critics in other areas contend that Jan Van Krimpen is probably one of the greatest book typographers of the 20th century.

## EARLY INTEREST WAS NOT DESIGN

He came to designing the physical properties of books through his deep and early interest in their intellectual properties. At about the age of 18 he became interested in the works of several young Dutch poets. These young literati would meet at coffee houses and each others' homes to discuss the merits of their and others' work. Though not a poet, Van Krimpen was drawn to this group. He felt a kinship with their passion for words and enjoyed the many hours of long, and at times animated, conversations he shared with

them. One of the poets, Albert Besnard, wrote in a memoir of his friendship with Van Krimpen, "It was really remarkable, we learnt to hate people we had never met."

Van Krimpen's interest in the book arts grew to include typography, lettering, and eventually typeface design. In 1912, he designed various pieces for a new Dutch magazine dedicated to raising the standards of typography and printing in Holland. The magazine had a relatively small but influential readership, and as a result helped to establish Van Krimpen's early reputation as a demanding, talented, and exceptionally conservative typographer. Much like Stanley Morison in England, whose writing and work had a profound influence on the young Dutch designer, Van Krimpen detested all forms of typographic ornamentation, or what he called, "typography for publicity." Later in life, he wrote, "I might say I have no particularly high regard for it (publicity) either; and that publicity—typographical and of any other variety—is apt to work with me the *not* intended way round."

Van Krimpen's enthusiasm for printing and the graphic arts was fired by a visit to a remarkable exhibition of the typographic arts in Leipzig in 1914. Viewing the displayed works was all the additional encouragement he needed. Upon his return to Holland, he opened a freelance design business specializing in designing and lettering for literary publications.

In 1917, he began to publish a series of small books of poetry, mostly written by his friends. These Palladium Books further helped to establish Van Krimpen's reputation as a designer and lettering artist.

## THE BIG BREAK

Van Krimpen worked at his freelance business for several years, eventually building up a healthy client base, and an impressive network of friends and associates. It was one such friend at the Dutch

THE GOSPEL ACCORDING TO SAINT JOHN
In the beginning was the Word, & the Word was with God, & the Word was God. The same was in the beginning with God. All things were made by him; & without him was not any thing made that was made. In him was life; and the life was the light of men. And the light shineth in darkness; and the darkness comprehended it not.

THE GOSPEL ACCORDING TO SAINT JOHN
In the beginning was the Word, and the Word was with God, and the Word was God. The same was in the beginning with God. All things were made by him; and without him was not any thing made that was made. In him was life; and the life was the light of men. And the light shineth in darkness; and the darkness comprehended it not.

Light. That was the true Light, which lighteth every man that cometh into the world. He was in the world, and the world was made by him, and the world knew him not. He came unto his own, and his own received him not. But as many as received him, to them gave he power to become the sons of God, even to them that believe on his name: Which were born, not of blood, nor

ROMANEÉ AND ROMANEÉ ITALIC

Post Office that provided Van Krimpen with the project that was to begin his career as a world-class type designer. In 1923, a special issue of stamps was being prepared for the 25th jubilee celebrating Queen Wilhelmina's accession to the Dutch throne, and the artist commissioned to create the stamp art, Von Konijnenburg, was having trouble with the lettering. Van Krimpen's friend was general secretary of the Dutch Post Office and suggested that the promising lettering artist be asked to help.

The prestigious printing house of Enschedé en Zonen printed the stamp, and Van Krimpen's lettering caught the attention of its director, Johannes Enschedé. The division of Enschedé's printing house that printed the stamp was very busy and quite profitable, but the book and letterpress side of the business had been allowed to deteriorate over the years. Dr. Enschedé figured that a new typeface by a talented young designer such as Van Krimpen might be just what this less successful side of the business needed to encourage new patrons. Van Krimpen was asked to design a new typeface for the firm, to be cut by P. H. Rädish, Enschedé's long-time employee and widely renowned punch cutter, and cast at the company's foundry. Van Krimpen eagerly accepted the commission and quickly produced trial drawings for the new type. These were approved and followed in record time with a set of finished renderings. The work was then handed over to Rädish, who produced punches for the handset type. In just over a year, from his first meeting with Van Krimpen, Dr. Enschedé had a font of type.

Part of the reason for the unusually quick turnaround on the development of the font was Dr. Enschedé's goal to use the new type for setting all the official entries for an international exhibition of industrial design to be held in Paris in 1925. He rightfully felt that this would provide both an excellent opportunity to announce the release of the new typeface and the perfect venue to gain maximum European market exposure. The finished design was called Lutetia, the Roman name for the city of Paris. Lutetia's release announcement in Paris did exactly what Enschedé had hoped.

## ALMOST UNANIMOUS APPROVAL

Stanley Morison reviewed the new face in *The Fleuron,* praising Van Krimpen's work as being fresh and original at a time when most new designs were copies, or revivals, of older work. *The Fleuron* article stated that Van Krimpen had "kept himself free from current . . . fashions," and that his design was "an exceedingly handsome one, its proportions . . . most agreeable." Dr. Enschedé was apparently equally pleased with the design because he hired Van Krimpen to create further typefaces for his company.

Not everybody, however, agrees with Mr. Morison and Dr. Enschedé. Walter Tracy, the eminent British typophile and former head of type design for the British Linotype Company, was almost gleeful in his criticism of Lutetia. It was his opinion that numerous letters in the design are out of proportion, poorly rendered, or inappropriate for the style of the face. Tracy also wrote that the italic was too distinctive to combine well with the roman, and that the alternative swash characters made for the italic "prettify the text only at the expense of comfortable reading." (Mr. Tracy clearly wasn't pulling any of *his* punches.) To give credit to Tracy, it is interesting that Van Krimpen, the conservative typographer, would create the swash characters in the first place; and many years later he did, in fact, write that he changed his mind and disapproved of the designs.

Upon close scrutiny, Tracy's criticisms are valid, but then type is intended to be used, viewed, and probably criticized when set in mass. A common comment about Caslon, for example, is that when taken individually, characters seem awkward or poorly shaped, but when set in text copy, the results are beautiful and ultimately readable (the total being greater than the sum of its parts).

To just about everyone but Tracy, Lutetia was a refreshing new addition to the typographic spectrum. It made Van Krimpen's reputation as a type designer,

and the types he created during the following 25 years were received with the greatest of respect.

## A CLOSE WORKING RELATIONSHIP

In addition to creating new types for Enschedé, Van Krimpen was also given the responsibility of designing the specimen sheet publicizing the printing house's range of historic and contemporary typefaces. He quickly earned an international reputation as a result of this work, which brought him additional projects at Enschedé, and the beginnings of a substantial freelance business. Over the years the relationship between Dr. Enschedé and Van Krimpen grew from one of employer-employee into a friendship of deep mutual respect and admiration. As a result, Van Krimpen remained associated with the Enschedé printing house until his death.

Like many other type designers, Van Krimpen didn't limit his freelance work to alphabets. He also drew several series of stamps, lettered numerous book jackets known for their elegance and simplicity, and wrote a number of articles, monographs, and lectures on type and typography.

Van Krimpen's status within Enschedé was molded by his own strength of character and personal goals. As a result, he never became a director of the firm, nor was he responsible for any major financial or operational decisions. Van Krimpen, however concentrated more on the artistic and creative aspects of Enschedé's business. He also acquired a great deal of liberty to work at home and to travel abroad. He became friendly with artists, poets, paper makers, printers, and publishers in the many countries in which he traveled extensively. He soon began to receive graphic design commissions from all over Europe. Some of his finest work was done for the Nonesuch Press and The Limited Editions Club in England, but his enthusiasm went beyond the limits of artistic and literary productions. He developed a great interest in liturgical printing, which further extended his travels to monasteries and religious printing houses in Europe and North Africa. Decades before travel by jet, fax machines, and overnight mail delivery, Van Krimpen had the same flexibility of client base and diversity of work as any modern graphic designer. Van Krimpen's reputation as a lettering artist, type designer, and calligrapher brought him many commissions. Apart from the numerous typefaces he created for the house of Enschedé, he also took on type design commissions from Bible printers, from the Monotype Corporation, and at the time of his death he was at work on a new alphabet for the Lumitype (later to become the Photon) phototypesetter.

## INTERNATIONAL ACCLAIM

As a result of his diverse and exceptional work, Van Krimpen received numerous honors within his lifetime. In his own country, the city of Amsterdam gave him its first award in typography in 1945. In England he received the gold medal of the Society of Industrial Artists in 1956. He was the first Dutchman to be elected an honorary member of the Double Crown Club in London. He joined Association Typographique Internationale shortly after its inaugural meeting in 1957 and played an active part in its affairs as a member of the board of directors.

Van Krimpen's second typeface was a Greek type called Antigone. Unfortunately, like Sophocles' heroine, for whom it is named, the design didn't reach old age. Antigone was intended to be the first part of a large type offering that would provide all the characters and symbols necessary to set mathematical textbooks. Unfortunately, only the alphabetical characters were produced (no numerals, punctuation, or any of the intended math symbols), which prevented any practical applications for the face. This is doubly unfortunate because his next Greek type, although completed, was not successful from a design standpoint. In Greek typesetting, traditionally the capital letters are roman (noncalligraphic) in design, while the correspond-

**LUTETIA ROMAN**

ABCDEFGHIJKLMN OPQRSTUVWXYZ

Irascimini, et nolite peccare: quæ dicitis in cordibus vestris, in cubilibus vestris compungimini. Sacrificate sacrificium iustitiæ, et sperate in Domino. Multi dicunt: Quis ostendit nobis bona? Signatum est super nos lumen vultus tui Domine: dedisti lætitiam in corde meo. A fructu frumenti, vini, et olei sui multiplicati sunt. In pace in idipsum dormiam, et requiescam; Quoniam tu Domine singulariter in spe constituisti me.

abcdefghijklmnopqrstuvwxyz
1234567890

LUTETIA ROMAN

**LUTETIA ITALIC**

*ABCDEFGHIJKLMN OPQRSTUVWXYZ*

*Irascimini, et nolite peccare: quæ dicitis in cordibus vestris, in cubilibus vestris compungimini. Sacrificate sacrificium iustitiæ, et sperate in Domino. Multi dicunt: Quis ostendit nobis bona? Signatum est super nos lumen vultus tui Domine: dedisti lætitiam in corde meo. A fructu frumenti, vini, et olei sui multiplicati sunt. In pace in idipsum dormiam, et requiescam; Quoniam tu Domine singulariter in spe constituisti me.*

*abcdefghijklmnopqrstuvwxyz*
*1234567890*

LUTETIA ITALIC

ΑΒΓΔΕΖΗΘΙΚΛΜΝ
ΞΟΠΡΣΤΥΦΧΨΩ

οὐ βραδύνει κύριος τῆς ἐπαγ-
γελίας, ὥς τινες βραδυτῆτα ἡγο-
ῦνται, ἀλλὰ μακροθυμεῖ εἰς ὑμᾶς,
μὴ βουλόμενός τινας ἀπολέσθαι
ἀλλὰ πάντας εἰς μετάνοιαν χω-
ρῆσαι. Ἥξει δὲ ἡμέρα κυρίου ὡς
κλέπτης, ἐν ᾗ οἱ οὐρανοὶ ῥοιζηδὸν
παρελεύσονται, στοιχεῖα δὲ καυ-
σούμενα λυθήσεται, καὶ γῆ καὶ τὰ
ἐν αὐτῇ ἔργα εὑρεθήσεται.

αβγδεζηθικλμνξοπρςστυφχψω

ANTIGONE

ing lowercase letters are cursive. Van Krimpen thought that this was all quite silly. "Why Greek scholars seem hardly to object to the combination of almost purely epigraphic capitals and clumsily calligraphic lowercase I have failed to understand. . . ." In his first Greek type, Van Krimpen followed tradition; in his second he did not.

Another short-circuited design by Van Krimpen in Romanée. It was drawn as a companion to an 18th-century italic punch cutters. Punches, matrices, and the tools necessary for creating fonts were still extant for the italic, and specimen showings were still intact for the original roman; but the punches and matrices for this latter face were long gone. Van Krimpen's goal was to revive the "missing" roman. The logical path to re-create the roman would have been to photographically enlarge the surviving prints of the roman type from the old specimen showings and use these as the foundation for renderings of the new design.

## THE OPERATION WAS A SUCCESS, HOWEVER, THE PATIENT DIED

But Van Krimpen didn't take the logical path. Perhaps because, as he later wrote, he didn't agree with the whole idea of type revivals, Van Krimpen chose to create a new roman design retaining only the proportions and basic features of the 18th-century original. This may have seemed like a good idea when the project began, but what Van Krimpen eventually produced had virtually no family resemblance to the face it was supposed to complement. The finished product was, even to Van Krimpen, a "distinct failure" as a companion to the ancient italic—although he did go on to claim that his design was just "too perfect" to complement the existing italic. Apparently, printers and typesetters agreed with the first part of Van Krimpen's critique more than the second, because after its initial release Romanée proceeded on pretty much a straight course to typographic obscurity.

Typefaces are often named for their designers, sometimes for loved ones, and once in a while after cities; rarely after a bottle of wine. Romanée is the exception. It seems that the christening for the typeface took place during a good dinner between Van Krimpen and the general manager of Monotype Corporation, at a well-known English country inn. The wine at dinner (more than a couple of bottles, as the story goes), a famous vintage Burgundy, Vosne-Romanée, was the high point of the meal. When the after-dinner discussion turned to the topic of Van Krimpen's new typeface, the logical name for the yet-unfinished design seemed obvious.

In 1932, Van Krimpen began work on a type family that was to be his most ambitious, innovative, and trouble-laden work. Several years prior to beginning the design, Van Krimpen met Stanley Morison, the typographic director of Monotype. The two men became close friends who respected each other's work, collaborated on several projects, and from time to time, enjoyed an argument—especially if it took place after a good meal. One of the subjects on which they did not argue was Morison's theory that the ideal basis for a typographic family was roman, sloped roman (as opposed to cursive italic), and a script (Chancery italic).

## AN EXTENDED FAMILY

The type family Van Krimpen started in 1932 acknowledged Morison's philosophy—and went him one better. In Van Krimpen's words, "When I started anew, I set out on what I think to have been a more ambitious scheme than, either before or since, has ever been tackled in the history of producing printing type. The idea was to create a complete type family comprising, to start with, roman, sloped roman, bold, and condensed bold, at least four weights of sans serif, a script type, and a number of Greek characters; I saw no reason then why it should be limited to what I have mentioned."

The design program began with work on the roman. Van Krimpen used the earlier Lutetia as the foundation for this type. In doing so, he hoped to correct some of the problems that he perceived in the previous design. "The lowercase of Lutetia being, on the whole, on the narrow side, it was to be expected that this new face should be wider. . . . A number of capitals of Lutetia were against the classical Roman tradition, too wide . . . ; their width has been reduced."

The first release in this extended family was met with enthusiasm. Everyone agreed that the design was a success. Van Krimpen was satisfied with his work, the typographic community was unanimous in their acceptance of the design, even Walter Tracy approved of the type—although he did feel obligated to qualify his opinion.

Design for Romulus "italic" was begun shortly after the roman was completed but was not released until 1936. This design followed Morison's theory of a sloped roman, rather than the much more traditional cursive style. The width of letters is only slightly more condensed

than that of the roman, and the alphabetical characters follow the roman shapes almost exactly. The resulting italic companion to the roman was released—with almost as much success as the 1958 Ford Edsel. (Wrong design, at the wrong time, and released for the wrong reasons to an unsympathetic consumer.)

As a result, more than six years after the original roman release, Romulus still had no text companion—at least no successful text companion.

## WHAT'S IN A NAME?

Third on Van Krimpen's priority list for Romulus was the "cursive." This design could have solved the "companionship" problem, but unfortuntely it also ran into trouble. First, there was probably the typeface name; Morison and Van Krimpen decided that the design should be patterned after a traditional calligraphic style, Cancelleresca Bastarda, and adopted this name for the face. (The correct pronunciation does not include the second "s," but only the more sophisticated type users are

---

ROMANÉE ROMAN

A B C D E F G H I J K L M N O P Q R S T U V W X Y Z

Irascimini, et nolite peccare: quæ dicitis in cordibus vestris, in cubilibus vestris compungimini. Sacrificate sacrificium iustitiæ, et sperate in Domino. Multi dicunt: Quis ostendit nobis bona? Signatum est super nos lumen vultus tui Domine: dedisti lætitiam in corde meo. A fructu frumenti, vini, et olei sui multiplicati sunt. In pace in idipsum dormiam, et requiescam; Quoniam tu Domine singulariter in spe constituisti me.

abcdefghijklmnopqrstuvwxyz
ctfbfffffiflfhfifkfl
1234567890

**ROMULUS ROMAN**

---

ROMULUS ROMAN

A B C D E F G H I J K L M N O P Q R S T U V W X Y Z

Irascimini, et nolite peccare: quæ dicitis in cordibus vestris, in cubilibus vestris compungimini. Sacrificate sacrificium iustitiæ, et sperate in Domino. Multi dicunt: Quis ostendit nobis bona? Signatum est super nos lumen vultus tui Domine: dedisti lætitiam in corde meo. A fructu frumenti, vini, et olei sui multiplicati sunt. In pace in idipsum dormiam, et requiescam; Quoniam tu Domine singulariter in spe constituisti me.

abcdefghijklmnopqrstuvwxyz
fbfffffiflfhfifkfl
1234567890

**ROMULUS SLOPED ROMAN**

aware of this.) Many feel that just the name of the face was too big a hurdle for most potential buyers to overcome.

Then, there are the swash letters. Again Morison and Van Krimpen discussed the design program and decided that a variety of swash and alternate characters should be offered with the face, to allow a reasonable amount of typographer latitude in producing composition that echoed calligraphic writing. The number of alternate characters they decided as reasonable proved, however, to be excessive by many standards. In addition to the basic alphabet, the typesetter who hoped to work with Cancelleresca Bastarda had to contend with over 90 swash and alternate letter. Difficult enough to handle with current computer aided digital typesetters, virtually impossible with handset type.

The third strike against Cancelleresca Bastarda was more technical in nature. Because the swash letters were designed with such flourish, the ascenders and descenders of the face were dramatically out of proportion with most other types. This meant that Cancelleresca Bastarda had to be cast on a point body 25 percent larger than the corresponding Romulus roman. A 25 percent increase in 8-point type adds up to 10 points, and a 25 percent larger 16-point type is 20 points—so far no problem for Romulus roman and the companion Cancelleresca Bastarda. (Here's where the trouble begins.) Twelve-point Romulus roman would require Cancelleresca Bastarda to be available at 15 point, not a standard size in metal type, and 10-point roman would yield a 12.5-point Cancelleresca Bastarda—clearly a real problem for any traditional typecasting. To make matters worse, if Cancelleresca Bastarda were to be used in conjunction with Romulus roman, then additional spacing material would have to be added above and below the roman words to make up the additional space required by the script—not an exciting proposition for busy compositors.

The end result was that Cancelleresca Bastarda could not function as part

CANCELLERESCA BASTARDA

of a type family but only as an attractive and difficult-to-use individual design. It was only with the introduction of 2-inch display setting film fonts, developed more than 35 years after Cancelleresca Bastarda's introduction, that the face got much actual use.

After Cancelleresca Bastarda, Van Krimpen created Semi Bold and Semi Bold Condensed versions of the roman design, and after these, a Greek version. None were commercial successes for the Enschedé type foundry.

## A LOGICAL GREEK

A serious flaw in the Greek design was that Van Krimpen tried to make it look as though it was directly related to Romulus roman. While this may sound logical in theory, the problem is that type design, many times, is not logical. Characters must look familiar, comfortable, to the intended reader. If the design is logically, rationally, correct but does not look right, then it isn't. Romulus Greek does, indeed look like Romulus roman—the problem is that it does not look like Greek type. (Nice design, but it didn't sell.)

A series of sans serif types based on the roman's proportions and basic design characteristics were also begun, but never finished. Twelve-point punches were cut, but no work was done beyond this early stage of development.

Romulus was a good idea; Sumner Stone proved this many years later with his "extended" ITC typeface family, but Van Krimpen's design was not executed in a manner that made it a viable product. Stone's was.

continued to visit the printing house and remained active in its business affairs. He died, as he had hoped, painlessly and while at work. He had just arrived one day at the entrance to Enschedé and was about to step out of the car, when he slumped back, collapsed in his seat, and died. He was 66.

Van Krimpen once wrote, "Everything that counts in typography is subtlety." He tried to incorporate this philosophy in all his work. He was, however, more successful in his typography than in his typeface design in meeting this goal.

## JUST A GOOD, SOLID DESIGN

Van Krimpen's most successful typeface is a design he initially created for a private publishing house for the production of a new Bible. The design brief called for a face that was exceptionally legible and easy on the eyes, and at the same time space economical. The finished product successfully met both criteria—and suffered from no technical or philosophical misdirections.

The face was named Spectrum, after the publishing house, and was cut as handset type by Rädish at the Enschedé foundry. Later in 1950, Monotype licensed the design from Enschedé and released it as a machine-set type.

Shortly before his death, Van Krimpen had begun work on a design that would have been one of the first original typefaces for photo composition. Had he completed the design, he would have been one of the very few designers to create original type for handset, machine-set metal, and phototypesetting equipment.

After his retirement from Enschedé en Zonen in 1957, Van Krimpen

## ARTISTS, CRAFTSPEOPLE, AND TYPEFACE DESIGN

Some critics have suggested that Van Krimpen was too much the artist, and others contend that he intellectualized too much. The end result was the same: Too much of Van Krimpen was apparent in his type designs. This made the finished product too much a personal statement rather than "anonymous" and totally functional communciations tools. History has proved that the best typefaces are those drawn by an inspired craftsperson or an artist who was able to sublimate the need to make a personal design statement. Van Krimpen was neither.

But his typography always looked right. Van Krimpen used his own types with greater distinction than did any of his peers. Graphic communicators throughout the world have reason to remember Van Krimpen and his work. He provided us with a rich heritage of original, if not totally uncontroversial, type designs, and excellent examples of how these and other typefaces are used best.

# Robert Hunter Middleton

## 1898–1985

ABCDEFGHIJK
abcdefghijklmnop
*ABCDEFGHIJKL*
*abcdefghijklmnopqr*
**ABCDEFGHIJ**
**abcdefghijklmn**

GARAMOND

During the 1930s, the Ludlow Typograph Company had, as its director of publicity, someone particularly flamboyant, arrogant, and decidedly egotistical. To describe him as being "difficult to work with" would be akin to calling *Tyrannosaurus rex* a big lizard. Douglas McMurtrie generally made life difficult for anyone who had the dubious privilege of working with him. In the entire typographic community, there was only one associate who escaped McMurtrie's wrath: R. Hunter Middleton.

Middleton drew typefaces for Ludlow and directed the company's type development program. He built the type library that McMurtrie publicized.

That McMurtrie and Middleton were never at odds was, at the very least, a tribute to the latter's tact and patience. It was because Middleton could relate to McMurtrie's artistic nature—his need for exposure and adulation—and was pragmatic enough not to allow personality differences to interfere with his job of building Ludlow's type library.

Middleton worked at Ludlow for nearly half a century. During that time he drew almost 100 typefaces and built the Ludlow type resource into one of the most respected font libraries in the world. He also helped to give substance and direction to the fledgling American graphic design community. Middleton was the early moving force behind a number of graphic and typographic organizations that have since become cornerstones of the graphic communications industry.

For many years the Ludlow Typograph Company built and sold a display composition machine for metal type. It cast solid line slugs like the Linotype, but from handset brass matrices. The Ludlow machine was as reliable as a padlock, inexpensive, and required little operational expense. Yet, although the market for typesetting machines was relatively small in the 1930s and 1940s, Ludlow Typograph was an extremely profitable little company. How could this be? Like razor blades for razors, Ludlow made its profits from the sale of fonts to those who used its linecasters. As a result,

R. Hunter Middleton was to a considerable degree, responsible for Ludlow's financial success.

## A "TOO CONVENIENT" JOB

Middleton was hired by Ludlow in 1923 on what he thought was a temporary basis. "It was just all too convenient to last," he once wrote. "I mean, not only that there should be such a rare job opportunity, but for it to be available in Chicago just at the time I needed employment. It was much too convenient and timely to be credible." His first years at the company were spent working primarily as a staff designer and as an assistant to Robert Wiebking, Ludlow's master punch cutter and matrix engraver. Although he recalls it with great fondness, the young Middleton probably didn't have a terribly exciting job. But Wiebking was a generous man who went to great lengths to teach the young Middleton about creating practical type designs and durable fonts. And it was through Wiebking that Middleton met Frederic Goudy, who became a lifelong friend.

Goudy helped Middleton to further appreciate a carefully planned type library, the value of exceptional design—and how to work with independent, opinionated, and at times cantankerous, type designers.

On his own, Middleton developed an acute sensitivity and appreciation of typeface history and the traditions of typographic communication.

When Ludlow appointed him director of type design in 1933, Robert Middleton was perfectly prepared to take on the task of building its type library. His unspoken goal was to build a growing resource that satisfied the needs of day-to-day typesetting and provided the graphic design community with an ongoing stream of new and innovative type styles from which to choose.

Under Middleton's direction, the type design department at Ludlow was not only involved in, but actually controlled, font production during all stages of development. He supervised the creation of typeface renderings, controlled the making of patterns from which the punches were made, he furnished the specifications for punch engraving, and gave final approval of the punches prior to matrices being struck. And finally, matrices could be released for sale only after the design department approved proofs made from type that was cast from the new matrices.

From 1933 to 1971, Robert Middleton directed the building and controlled the quality of the Ludlow type library. He was, quite literally, the motivating force behind Ludlow type. When he retired, phototype was beginning to replace metal composition, and the Ludlow Company was unable to make the transition from one technology to the other. When Middleton left Ludlow, the company's type development program virtually ceased to exist.

## A Change in Career Path

Middleton wanted to be an artist—a painter. He began serious study to prepare for this career at the Art Institute of Chicago, but soon found another career path. While at the Institute, Middleton met an instructor who was to have a profound influence on his professional life.

The Art Institute of Chicago engaged Ernst Detterer as an instructor, with the intention of creating a new curriculum in the printing and typographic arts. He was a scholar, an artist, and a craftsman—all of which Middleton was later to become. Detterer studied in England, for a brief time under Edward Johnston. He had traveled widely prior to his appointment at the Art Institute, and acquired a deep reverence for the artistic achievement of the past. At the same time, he knew and admired the best contemporary work in Europe and America; a perfectionist, he set high standards for himself and for his students.

Middleton often referred to Detterer as the single most important influence on his professional career. He started by taking just one of the classes Detterer offered. Soon that course led to another, and then another. Before long, Middleton's teacher became his mentor, the young scholar decided against becoming a painter, and changed his course of study to lettering and type design.

Middleton's first typeface was, in fact, a project for which Detterer invited his assistance. The management at Ludlow had heard of Detterer's work at the Art Institute, and in 1923 commissioned him to develop a type based on Jenson's 15th-century font. Detterer worked from the same master design that Bruce Rogers used for Centaur years earlier, but his was to be more of an exact rendition of the original rather than a modern interpretation. Detterer had his promising student study the Jenson types as part of his curriculum and was so impressed with his ability and enthusiasm that he asked him to assist in the design of the Ludlow face. Middleton was delighted at the opportunity but had no idea that this would lead to his first job and a lifelong career. "Although I enjoyed helping Detterer it never occurred to me that there might be such a job on a permanent basis. After all, how many type designers were there in the world then—ten, maybe fifteen at the most?"

The result of the Detterer and Middleton design collaboration was a 16-point revival of Jenson's type called "Eusebius"—and a strong recommendation from Detterer that the promising type designer be given a job at Ludlow.

Ludlow did hire Middleton, and set as one of his first responsibilities the completion of the work begun by him and Detterer. (This was, of course, under the very close supervision of Wiebking.) A little over a year later, several point sizes were added to the roman font, and italic, bold, and bold italic versions were created to complement the initial designs. At this same time, Middleton also completed the renderings for his first original type design: Ludlow Black. This face, like many of Middleton's, was drawn as a direct competitor to popular faces from other foundries. In this case, the compet-

ABCDEFGHI
abcdefghijkln
*ABCDEFGHI*
*abcdefghijkln*
**ABCDEFGH**
**abcdefghijk**

RECORD GOTHIC

ing foundry was Barnhard Brothers & Spindler, and the design was the very popular Cooper Black. There are obvious similarities between the two designs, but Middleton's version is in many ways a more traditional and more successful (from a design standpoint) typeface. Its serifs are more conventional, its general color more consistent, and its character proportions more uniform than its direct competition. Unfortunately, it never came close to reaching the popularity of Oswald Cooper's powerhouse.

Over the years he worked at Ludlow, Middleton became a master at both the art and craft of type design. Ludlow was a young company in the 1920s, when Middleton began working there. To become competitive with the more established type suppliers like Monotype, Linotype, and American Type Founders, Ludlow required a type library that provided new and original designs, as well as types that served as functional equivalents to the established workhorse fonts of those more senior vendors. Middleton provided Ludlow with both. He produced many new and truly original designs that established Ludlow as a major player in the industry for over thirty years. He also became a master at rendering beautiful "alternative" designs: typefaces that blended proven and popular design traits with enough originality to classify the end results as fresh—and much more than mere copies.

The Tempo, Record Gothic, and Karnak families are Middleton creations aimed at countering similar designs from other foundries. Middleton's Garamond and Bodoni are scholarly interpretations of these now generic type styles. In addition, Middleton was responsible for sev-

eral thoroughly original types. His Stellar is a calligraphic sans that predates Optima by more than 20 years; and Radiant is another sans unlike any that preceded it. Other originals by Middleton include scripts like Coronet, Admiral, and Florentine; the elegant caps-only Delphian Open Titling; and such display faces a Eden, Samson, and Lafayette.

## TWO SPECIAL DESIGNS

Middleton's Garamond and Stellar deserve special recognition. At the turn of the century, many foundries were reviving the types of Claude Garamond, some based their designs on the original 16th-century work of the French type designer; most, however, used Jean Jannon's 17th-century interpretation of Garamond's fonts.

Middleton chose yet another foundation for his work. His Garamond is an exceptionally beautiful and scholarly revival of the Garamond and Granjon types shown in the Conrad Berner specimen showing of 1592. Middleton's design is more calligraphic and generally more delicate than other Garamonds—the italic being an especially elegant design, with refined character spacing unmatched by the Garamond italics offered from Ludlow's competitors.

When other foundries were releasing geometric sans serif typefaces like Kabel, Futura, and Spartan, Middleton countered with Ludlow's functional equivalent, Tempo. Tempo is a geometric sans that most would be hard pressed to distinguish from Futura or Spartan. It is a yeoman design that is technically equal to its competition, but clearly not superior in design or refinement. Tempo

RENDERS THE LUDLOW
system particularly worthy of the

allowed Ludlow to remain in the typeface fashion game, and Stellar was Middleton's attempt to raise the ante.

Stellar is a less severe sans than its geometric cousins, aimed at providing graphic designers with a transitional step between the strict geometrics of faces like Futura, and more the traditional roman serifed designs. Middleton based Stellar on oldstyle proportions: modest x-height, wide caps, and a subtle contrast between thick and thin. Where classic oldstyle designs have serifs, Middleton substituted a flaring of the character stroke. The result looks a little like a blend of Kabel and Optima with just a dash of Syntax—released, however, more than 30 years before either of the latter two designs.

Ludlow cut Stellar in a full range of point sizes, but the family was unfortunately limited to just roman and bold designs. They sold moderately well but gained nowhere near the popularity of the stressed sans that followed it.

Record Gothic is perhaps Middleton's most successful sans serif family. Begun in 1927 as an alternative to other foundries' 19th-century grotesques like Venus and Standard, it, as with the Stellar, was released in only a minimum of weights. Then in the late 1950s, Middleton used these as the foundation for a much larger family to compete with the likes of Helvetica and Univers. In many ways, Record Gothic is a more accurate translation of the 19th-century grotesque style than either Helvetica or Univers. It has the traditional bowl and loop "g," condensed letter proportions, and 90-degree-cut terminals found in faces like Franklin Gothic and News Gothic. The unfortunate aspect is that, although more accurate, these traits also tend, by current fashions, to make the face look a little old-fashioned.

By the time he retired in 1971, Middleton had created almost 100 typefaces for the Ludlow Typograph Company. Some, like Stellar and Radiant, were absolutely original in their designs. Others were his interpretation of what have now become almost generic styles.

In every face, whether revival, functional equivalent, or original, Middleton, however, imparted an honesty and strength to his designs. Middleton was one of that rare breed of type designer—both artist and craftsperson.

## NOT ALL ARTISTS PAINT PICTURES

Most of us, except for an occasional desire to emulate a childhood hero, grow up without a sense of how we will spend our adult years. Not so for Robert Middleton; from his earliest recollections he knew that he wanted to be an artist. He may not have been exactly sure what it meant to be an artist, but he was sure that his gift of being able to draw well, and something which he wasn't yet able to label as creativity, would play an active role in his adult life.

But there was another influence on the young Middleton's life; and some feel that this may have precluded him from becoming the kind of artist he first hoped to be—and perhaps even stunted his growth as a type designer.

He had grown up in a hard-working Scottish family. His father was a conservative, practical, and very successful businessman. Some of this conservatism and practicality surely rubbed off on the young Middleton—and tempered his creativity. As a result, in his adult life he tended to think of himself more as a craftsperson than as an artist. At times Middleton even deprecated his natural creative talents.

He wanted to be a painter, and moved to Chicago shortly after high school to study at the Art Institute of Chicago. But he found that there were other students who were better painters, and his practical side told him to look for a more conservative and predictable career choice. Fortunately for the graphics community, he chose type. But even in his type design, Middleton was always the prudent practitioner rather than the flamboyant artist. He once confided in a close

ABCDEFGHIJK
abcdefghijklm
**ABCDEFGHIJ**
**abcdefghijkl**
ABCDEFGHIJKLMNO
abcdefghijklmnop

RADIANT

ABCDEFGHIJKLMNOPQRSTUVWXYZ&
abcdefghijklmnopqrstuvwxyz
1234567890$

TEMPO

ABCDEFGHIJKLMNOPQRSTUVWXY
abcdefghijklmnopqrstuvwxyz
1234567890

ABCDEFGHIJKLMNOPQRSTUVWXYZ
abcdefghijklmnopqrstuvwxyz

RECORD GOTHIC

friend, "I have never felt that my role was to create great personal typefaces. I never intended to follow the role of my friend Fred Goudy, or of Bruce Rogers. I was employed by a corporation and given a great deal of freedom, but I also felt a responsibility to their particular needs and to the needs of their customers."

And yet it is, in all likelihood, precisely those attributes which tempered his creative input that enabled Middleton to produce such a successful type library. Middleton wasn't developing typefaces for himself—he was developing them for others. His work wasn't necessarily a personal statement, but the process of building a practical and efficient set of tools for others to use.

Born in Scotland, he emigrated to America at the age of 10 with the rest of his family to join his father, who had secured a job managing a coal mine in Alabama. Several years later, the Middletons moved to Eldorado, Illinois, and then finally settled in Danville. He grew up like many boys in the first part of this century, having had a relatively undistinguished childhood—except, of course, for the part about his future goals.

After studying at the Chicago Academy of Fine Art for just a little over a month, he transferred to the Art Institute of Chicago, which offered a wider number of choices of study that could lead to a career in the arts. It is also where he was to meet Ernst Detterer.

Ludlow hired Middleton when he was 25. He devoted his entire professional life to the Ludlow Company, retiring in 1971 at the age of 73.

During his career at Ludlow, Middleton created one of America's most re-spected type libraries, designing almost 100 of the faces in the library himself. He was also dedicated to supporting and improving the industry in which he worked. He was instrumental in founding and developing the Chicago-based Society of Typographic Arts, active in organizations such as the Typographers, and the Type Designers Club. In addition, he was one of the first Americans to join and help build the international typographic association of Association Typographique Internationale (A.Typ.I.), which was one of the first proponents of typeface design protection. Middleton was also one of the founders of the Aspen International Designs Conference, and was a primary force in organizing many of its early meetings. Living proof of the adage. "If you want something done, give it to a busy person," Middleton also found time to write numerous books and articles on type, typography, and type design, and to run a small, unprofitable but prolific, private press in his basement.

Middleton died in 1985, leaving a legacy that is a vital part of American typographic heritage. He was important, but by choice he was not famous. History tends to honor the famous and not the important. In his time, few people knew of R. Hunter Middleton; today there are even fewer. Once the type designer Rudolf Koch asked Victor Hammer, another designer and friend of Middleton's, "Who is Robert Middleton?" The reply summed up the man. "For an artist, he is too practical minded, too sober, too normal; there is nothing fanciful or exalted about him For a craftsman, his interests are too broad, his understanding is too profound."

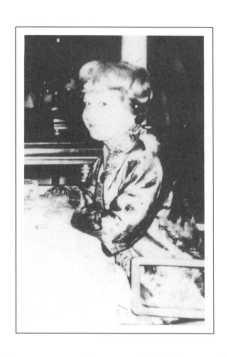

*Beatrice Warde*

1900–1969

On a cool night in October of 1928, Ms. Beatrice Warde delivered the first speech by a woman to that prestigious, tradition-bound—and male-dominated—British printing society, The Worshipful Company of Stationers. For the occasion at Stationers' Hall, she wore a black chiffon evening dress studded with black crystal beads and highlighted by a large orchid pinned to her shoulder. Ms. Warde, who had not yet reached the age of 30, was both honored and thrilled by the opportunity to speak before such an august group. She was not, however, overwhelmed.

Her plan was to take advantage of the occasion. The dress was for drama. She wanted to shock the society members just a little—to be sure that they noticed and paid attention to her. No props, however, were necessary. The young Ms. Warde was drama enough for the staid printers in attendance. In her short talk, she managed to chide, challenge, poke fun at—and completely charm—her audience.

## A WOMAN NOT
## TO BE UNDERESTIMATED

For most of her career, the title on Beatrice Warde's business card read "Director of Publicity, British Monotype Corporation." This doesn't, however, begin to describe the breadth and value of her responsibilities and influence within Monotype, or her contributions to the typographic community. Early in her career, Beatrice discovered (as other creative and individualistic people within corporate environments have discovered) that if you are willing to waive a climb to the top of the corporate ladder, a surprising amount of freedom can be at your disposal—enhanced by corporate support. While she never rose above a middle-management position at Monotype, Beatrice Warde's influence on typography and typographers was, in many cases, more pronounced and far-reaching than that of the corporate officers.

## STATIONER'S HALL,
## 32 YEARS LATER

In 1960 Ms. Warde was asked, once again, to speak at Stationers' Hall—this time, on the occasion of her 60th birthday. Toward the end of that talk (which was considerably longer—and gentler—than her first), Beatrice confessed, "Work has been a game all my life. It's been more fun than I could possibly tell you. It has been like being in love. . . ."

## A LIFE'S COMMITMENT
## TO EDUCATION

In that same 60th-birthday talk at Stationers' Hall, those in attendance were reminded of one of Ms. Warde's lifelong passions: her commitment to education and those who hold the future of typographic communication. "One of my most treasured birthday presents is from the first year apprentices of the Dundee School of Printing. These are boys of 15, who having to set the first line of type that their fingers would ever set in the course of their lives, took a week beforehand, each of them, in composing his own felicitous greeting to me . . . they are printed one under another in this birthday broadsheet. And I can tell you that when I got to the line by one, Edward Mitchell, 'This is my opening line —life's work begun'; I burst into joyful tears."

Beatrice began to visit printing schools, talking to and lecturing students, shortly after she started working for Monotype in 1925. She continued this service tirelessly for more than 30 years—even after she retired from other active work. The visits were more than likely Beatrice's idea rather than Monotype's, and she probably sold the company on the plan by presenting it as a solid business investment toward future type sales and use. Her personal goals were, however, undoubtedly more aesthetic than fiscal in nature. She believed fervently in the value of beautiful and effective typographic

"Imagine that you have before you a flagon of wine. You may choose your own favourite vintage for this imaginary demonstration, so that it be a deep shimmering crimson in colour. You have two goblets before you. One is of solid gold, wrought in the most exquisite patterns. The other is of crystal-clear glass, thin as a bubble, and as transparent. Pour and drink; and according to your choice of goblet, I shall know whether or not you are a connoisseur of wine. For if you have no feelings about wine one way or the other, you will want the sensation of drinking the stuff out of a vessel that may have cost thousands of pounds; but if you are a member of that vanishing tribe, the amateurs of fine vintages, you will choose the crystal, because everything about it is calculated to reveal rather than to hide the beautiful thing which it was meant to contain. ❖ Bear with me in this long-winded and fragrant metaphor; for you will find that almost all the virtues of the perfect wine-glass have a parallel in typography. There is the long, thin stem that obviates fingerprints on the bowl. Why? Because no cloud must come between your eyes and the fiery heart of the liquid. Are not the margins on book pages similarly meant to obviate the necessity of fingering the type-page? Again: the glass is colourless or at the most only faintly tinged in the bowl, because the connoisseur judges wine partly by its colour and is impatient of anything that alters it. There are a thousand mannerisms in typography that are as impudent and arbitrary as putting port in tumblers of red or green glass! When a goblet has a base that looks too small for security, it does not matter how cleverly it is weighted; you feel nervous lest it should tip over. There are ways of setting lines of type which may work well enough, and yet keep the reader subconsciously worried by the fear of 'doubling' lines, reading three words as one, and so forth. ❖ Printing demands a humility of mind, for the lack of which many of the fine arts are even now floundering in self-conscious and maudlin experiments. There is nothing simple or dull in achieving the transparent page. Vulgar ostentation is twice as easy as discipline. When you realise that ugly typography never effaces itself, you will be able to capture beauty as the wise men capture happiness by aiming at something else. The 'stunt typographer' learns the fickleness of rich men who hate to read. Not for them are long breaths held over serif and kern, they will not appreciate your splitting of hair-spaces. Nobody (save the other craftsmen) will appreciate half your skill. But you may spend endless years of happy experiment in devising that crystalline goblet which is worthy to hold the vintage of the human mind." ❖

CRYSTAL GOBLET ESSAY.

communication. She knew that the printing students she spoke to one day would be typographic practitioners the next. Beatrice wanted to share her enthusiasm and knowledge with these young apprentices.

## It All Started at ATF

Although it is through her association with Monotype that Beatrice Warde is best known, this was not the only typographic company to employ her talents. She first worked with the American Type Founders Company in New Jersey. It was here, in fact, that she began to build the foundation of knowledge on type and typography that would serve as the source for her later famous articles and lectures.

Aside from creating typefaces, printer's tools, and a variety of other products for the graphic arts, ATF also maintained a typographical library and printing museum tucked away in a particularly inhospitable and infrequently visited section of Jersey City. Beatrice was the assistant librarian for the library. For some, this could have been a boring and tedious job, but not for the inquisitive Ms. Warde. She delighted in the opportunity to work in such (to her) auspicious and intellectually stimulating surroundings. Henry Bullen (her immediate manager and ATF's librarian) only added to the opportunity: The first day of work he told her, "There are over 1,400 books in this library. I want you to dust them all—they collect dust on the tops. I don't *mind* [he added] if you stop to read the books."

Beatrice needed no further encouragement.

Prophetically, Henry Bullen also provided Warde with the topic for her first important article. While showing her a specimen of ATF's version of Garamond, he told her, "You know, this is definitely not a 16th-century type. It is based upon the type at the Imprimerie Nationale, which is itself *attributed* to Garamond, but I have never found a 16th-century book which contained this typeface. Anyone who discovers where this thing came from will make a great reputation."

And so it was.

## PROPHESY FULFILLED

Shortly after she left ATF and moved to England, Beatrice began working with Stanley Morison on *The Fleuron* magazine. One afternoon, while gathering information for an article, in a local museum, Beatrice discovered a title page with the familiar Garamond types, but with the imprint of Jean Jannon of Sedan. Pausing only to look up Jannon in the available reference books, she caught the night boat to Paris, went directly to the Mazarine library there, where she made the discovery that solved the Garamond puzzle. A telegram was immediately dispatched to Stanley Morison: "JANNON SPECIMEN SIMPLY GORGEOUS SHOWS ALL SIZES HIS TYPES WERE APPROPRIATED BY RAPACIOUS PAPIST GOVERNMENT HOORAY. . . ."

Jannon was a type founder who, in 1621, published the specimen showing that which Beatrice had discovered— showing types that were close copies of the earlier designs of Claude Garamond. As a result of this find, she was able to write her now-famous article on Garamond and fulfill Bullen's prophecy. The article, which ran 48 pages in the fifth edition of *The Fleuron,* did, indeed, as Bullen predicted, firmly establish Ms. Warde's

reputation as a typographic scholar. The deserved recognition, unfortunately, was not immediately forthcoming.

## MR. PAUL BEAUJON— WRITER AND HISTORIAN

Beatrice Warde's first writings were published under a male pseudonym. When asked later, she provided three reasons for this choice: First, her husband, Frederic, had already published a book about Bruce Rogers, and Beatrice thought it would be better not to have two Wardes writing about things typographic; second, her mother had made the name Becker well known in literary circles, so Beatrice chose not to use her maiden name; and finally, according to Beatrice (and anyone else who could be prompted to give an honest answer), nobody at that time would have accepted the fact that, "a woman could know anything about printing, typography, and such-like." So, by the time the Garamond article was published, she had already decided to write under the name of Paul Beaujon.

Through Beatrice's help, Mr. Beaujon became quite famous. So famous in fact, that he received fan mail. One very important letter was sent to him, in care of *The Fleuron,* by the head of the Lanston Monotype Company. He wrote to Mr. Beaujon inviting him to become editor of *The Monotype Recorder* magazine. He and the other executives at Monotype were clearly impressed with Mr. Beaujon's literary and scholarly abilities. They felt that his services could improve the quality of their own typographic magazine. Paul Beaujon wrote back to Monotype saying that he would be delighted to take the job, and in fact would be able to start working within a few weeks. The Monotype executives were more than a little surprised when "he" showed up at their offices at the appointed time. According to Beatrice, "They had never hired a woman in their

THIS IS
A PRINTING OFFICE

꙳

CROSSROADS OF CIVILIZATION

REFUGE OF ALL THE ARTS
AGAINST THE RAVAGES OF TIME

ARMOURY OF FEARLESS TRUTH
AGAINST WHISPERING RUMOUR

INCESSANT TRUMPET OF TRADE

FROM THIS PLACE WORDS MAY FLY ABROAD
NOT TO PERISH ON WAVES OF SOUND
NOT TO VARY WITH THE WRITER'S HAND
BUT FIXED IN TIME HAVING BEEN VERIFIED IN PROOF

FRIEND YOU STAND ON SACRED GROUND

THIS IS A PRINTING OFFICE

"THIS IS A PRINTING OFFICE"
BROADSHEET, SET IN MONOTYPE
PERPETUA

place above the rank of secretary and had no idea how to deal with 'her'! But I got . . . the job with use of a secretary and part of a desk."

## NEVER IDLE

Perhaps Ms. Warde needed her two personalities to accomplish everything she wanted. In addition to her responsibilities at *The Monotype Recorder,* she was a prolific writer of a variety of subjects (from the effects of television on our society to the cartoonist Walt Kelly); she was continually called upon to speak at conferences and seminars; she found time for design commissions; she even began to take over the responsibilities of all Monotype's type publicity and public relations. These last were tasks which Stanley Morison had previously undertaken, but which he began to relinquish to the more vivacious and energetic Ms. Warde. Morison created scholarly documents, conservatively designed brochures, and *The*

*Monotype Recorder;* Beatrice produced posters, advertisements, specimen booklets, and *The Monotype Newsletter.* They complemented each other perfectly.

## THE FIRST LADY OF TYPOGRAPHY

More than once, Beatrice Warde has been referred to as the "First Lady of Typography"—and not just because she wrote articles and gave lectures on the subject. She was also an accomplished typographer. The talent was probably always there, but her position as director of publicity for Monotype forced her to exercise and refine the talent. The responsibilities of her position meant that not only creative marketing concepts fell under her jurisdiction; so did copywriting, graphic design, and production control. As an example, Ms. Warde first conceived of the idea of *The Monotype Newsletter* as a marketing tool. She then edited it, wrote much of the copy, designed the typeface announcement pages, and even produced much of the cover art.

Probably her most famous typographic effort was a broadside she developed in one afternoon to showcase Eric Gill's titling version of the Perpetua family. The idea was to show every point size the typeface was released in, and in a manner that was so attractive that people would be compelled to frame and hang the piece. Her "This is a Printing Office" is the end result. One of the criteria Ms. Warde placed before herself was to make the finished piece as universally applicable as possible. In her words "as the broadsheet is to hang on the walls of printing offices, it might as well be an inscription for a printing office. But whatever it says will have to be true of *any* place where printing is done. . . . It cannot talk about handsome typefaces, intelligent proofreading, exquisite craftsmanship in makeready. It will also have to say honestly and accurately what can be said about the smallest, grimiest, most nearly comical

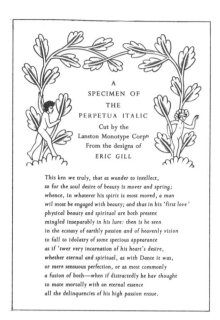

FIRST PROOF OF PERPETUA ITALIC.
COPY WRITTEN BY PAUL BEAUJON
(BEATRICE WARDE).

little steam printer in any suburban side street."

The end result was absolutely successful—as a design and as a marketing tool. The words Beatrice chose and the typography she produced are particularly elegant solutions to the design problem. "This is a Printing Office" hung in virtually every printing establishment in England, the clean and the grimy. It was reproduced several times, by Monotype, other companies, and individuals, and even cast in bronze to be hung on the wall at the entrance to the largest printing office in the world—that of the United States Government.

## MATTERS TYPOGRAPHIC

As successful as "This is a Printing Office" was, Beatrice Warde is remembered more for what she said and wrote about type rather than the typography she produced. In fact, her "crystal goblet" lecture to the British Typographers Guild gave us some of the most famous words ever spoken about typographic communication. Her metaphor, and the logical argument it evokes, is not only brilliant wordsmithing, it is also sound advice. The text of the first two, and last, paragraphs is provided here. They afford a glimpse into the exceptional powers of communication Ms. Warde possessed. The paragraphs are worth reading—remembering—and using as a foundation for all graphic communication.

"Imagine that you have before you a flagon of wine. You may choose your own favourite vintage for this imaginary demonstration, so that it be a deep shimmering crimson in colour. You have two goblets before you. One is of solid gold, wrought in the most exquisite patterns. The other is of crystal-clear glass, thin as a bubble, and as transparent. Pour and drink; and according to your choice of goblet, I shall know whether or not you are a connoisseur of wine. For if you have no feelings about wine one way or the other, you will want the sensation of drinking the stuff out of a vessel that may have cost thousands of pounds; but if you are a member of that vanishing tribe, the amateurs of fine vintages, you will choose the crystal, because everything about it is calculated to reveal rather than to hide the beautiful thing which it was meant to contain.

Bear with me in this long-winded and fragrant metaphor; for you will find that almost all the virtues of the perfect wine-glass have a parallel in typography. There is the long, thin stem that obviates fingerprints on the bowl. Why? Because no cloud must come between your eyes and the fiery heart of the liquid. Are not the margins on book pages similarly meant to obviate the necessity of fingering the type-page? Again: The glass is colourless or at the most only faintly tinged in the bowl, because the connoisseur judges wine partly by its colour and is impatient of anything that alters it. There are a thousand mannerisms in typography that are as impudent and arbitrary as putting port in tumblers of red or green glass! When a goblet has a base that looks too small for security, it does not matter how cleverly it is weighted; you feel nervous lest it should tip over. There are ways of setting lines of type which may work well enough, and yet keep the reader subconsciously worried by the fear of 'doubling' lines, reading three words as one, and so forth.

Printing demands a humility of mind, for the lack of which many of the fine arts are even now floundering in self-conscious and maudlin experiments. There is nothing simple or dull in achieving the transparent page. Vulgar ostentation is twice as easy as discipline. When you realise that ugly typography never effaces itself, you will be able to capture beauty as the wise men capture happiness by aiming at something else. The 'stunt typographer' learns the fickleness of rich men who hate to read. Not for them are long breaths held over serif and kern, they will not appreciate your splitting of hair-spaces. Nobody (save the other craftsmen) will appreciate half your skill. But you may spend endless years of happy experiment in devising that crystalline goblet which is worthy to hold the vintage of the human mind."

## "I Am a Communicator"

One of the things Beatrice Warde liked best, what she believed to be her greatest personal strength, was oral communication. She once said, "What I'm really good at is standing up in front of an audience with no preparation at all and then for 50 minutes refusing to let them even wriggle an ankle."

She was a performer: Her deep voice and seemingly boundless energy captivated audiences. It was difficult not to get caught up in her passion and enthusiasm.

## Education— The Foundation

Beatrice's early education was provided at home by her grandmother, who had formerly been the head of a private school. When she was 12, Beatrice went to one of New York's most progressive high schools. From there she went to Barnard College, where she says that she first developed a great interest in calligraphy and letterforms. She also developed a great interest in Frederic Warde. Frederic was one of typography's rising stars at the time, and it was through him that she was able to land her first job after college—and continue her education.

Frederic was a close friend of Bruce Rogers, the eminent American typographer and type designer. When Beatrice graduated from college, Rogers told her, "I will give you a letter to Henry Lewis Bullen—he's looking for an assistant librarian." When she turned up at Bullen's office at ATF, she found Bullen behind his desk, which had a large pile of correspondence from applicants for the assistant librarian position. Beatrice recalls, "Bullen said to me, 'Miss Becker, here is a stack of letters applying for this job—about 90; and they are all from qualified professional librarians. What have you got? You've got a letter from Bruce Rogers. You get the job.' I rejoiced!"

## The Meeting of a Lifetime

It was while she was working at ATF that Beatrice met Stanley Morison—an event that was to change both their lives. She learned that the already-famous Typographical Advisor to Monotype Corporation was planning a visit to the United States. Beatrice wrote him, inviting him to stay at her and Frederic's house when he was in the area. Morison declined the offer, but this did not discourage Beatrice. She learned that Morison planned to visit the typographic historian Daniel Updike, at his office in Boston. If Morison could not come to her, she would go to him. The train ride, several hours long, was a small price to pay to meet the famous Mr. Morison.

She recalls that important meeting: "I know that the stranger must be Morison. He looked like a Jesuit, with his black looks, black suit and blue jaw. And when he turned to see who was coming into the room his momentary frown of curiosity brought his heavy black eyebrows together with formidable effect. What I was not prepared for was the way that austere face, sombre in repose, could be instantly transfigured by a most captivating schoolboy grin. . . . Within the five minutes of the general conversation that followed I knew that I was in the presence not only of a wit and a scholar, but of a personality more vivid and stimulating than that of anyone I'd ever before encountered." A romantic would call Beatrice Warde's first meeting with Mr. Morison love at first sight.

Apparently Morison was equally impressed. He wrote to Beatrice upon his return to London, and soon thereafter he invited her and Frederic to come to England to work with him on a number of typographic projects. Beatrice was thrilled by the offer. Frederic wasn't so sure.

## Europe—New Work, New Challenges

Early in 1925, Beatrice and Frederic Warde arrived in Europe. Frederic Warde and Morison immediately began working on the projects Morison had described. They shared office space in London and proved to be a formidable creative team. Frederic also began to take on work of his own. He became quite busy and equally successful. Work and travel took up much of his time—leaving less and less time for Beatrice.

Beatrice and Frederic had agreed early in their marriage that each should be free to choose their own way of life. So when Frederic became busy building his career in England and Europe, Beatrice became more involved in the typographic business in London. She, much to the disfavor of his wife, began to do research for Stanley Morison.

Mable Morison has been described by several writers as being somewhat hysterical in her attitude toward the early relationship between her husband and the younger Ms. Warde. While she may have been excessive in her emotional reactions toward Beatrice, she also was no dummy. There was definitely something going on.

In the spring of 1925, Beatrice began to accompany Morison on a number of his business trips. Her "open" marriage with Frederic soon began to feel the strain. She, Frederic, and Morison tried to avoid the obvious for several months, but there was no deviating this juggernaut. Tension countinued to grow amongst the trio. Then, in the summer of 1926, it erupted with the inevitable terrible results. Personal and professional lives were thrown asunder. Late in November of that year, Beatrice, now separated from Frederic, went back to the United States for an extended stay. A few days later, Frederic, angry and dejected, picked up and left London, never to return. It was the end of their life together.

The following summer, Beatrice did return to London—to accept the job of editor of *The Monotype Recorder,* which was offered to Paul Beaujon. Two years later she was made head of Monotype's publicity department. The rest of her life, apart from short trips to the United States and continental Europe, was spent in England.

## Never Tiring

Many of us are exuberant, enthusiastic, and passionate in our twenties and thirties. As we grow older, the tendency is for our passions to cool down, our exuberance to mellow. One quality of greatness is a seemingly unending fountain of enthusiasm.

Enthusiasm came naturally to Beatrice. She was tireless in her desire to share her passions for type and typography with printers, students, and the reading public. She shared Bullen's vision of the importance of typographical education. Her own vision was enriched and broadened through her collaboration with Stanley Morison. Her generosity and natural ability to communicate only added to the wealth of her contribution.

## Too Soon Over

Beatrice Warde died on a Sunday in the middle of September. She had spent the day working in her garden; the afternoon turned cool and Beatrice had gone inside to build a fire. In the process of gathering the kindling, she collapsed. Death was instantaneous. Beatrice was 69.

At her memorial service, John Dreyfus, the eminent British typographer and historian, read from St. Paul's First Epistle to Timothy. The words are particularly appropriate to eulogize Ms. Warde:

*"Charge them that are rich in this world, that they be not highminded, nor trust in uncertain riches, but in the living God, who givith us richly all things to enjoy; that they do good, that they may be rich in good works, ready to distribute, willing to communicate."* 1 Timothy 6: 17–18

# Jan Tschichold
## 1902–1974

To look at him, you might think that he was a kindly professor of Latin, or perhaps classical literature. Jan Tschichold appears to be a scholarly, gentle man. Certainly not someone given to harsh words or radical thought.

True to his image, Jan Tschichold was a scholar and an educator. He wrote over 50 books and spent much of his free time teaching. His educational contribution was not, however, in Latin or Greek. Tschichold's expertise was in typography and typographic communication. However, antithetical to his image, much of his work was quite radical. And to muddy the picture even further, Tschichold was guilty of contradicting himself on some very basic issues.

## TSCHICHOLD THE REVOLUTIONARY

In the early part of this century, Jan Tschichold revolutionized typography by virtually single-handedly making asymmetric typographic arrangement the style of choice among young designers. In doing so he also vehemently attacked symmetry as being an archaic and ineffectual typographic style. Twenty-five years later, Tschichold began the Herculean task of redesigning, and restyling, the complete library of Penguin Books. By the time he was done, more than 500 titles had been reworked—almost every one of them arranged typographically symmetrical!

When he was young, Tschichold drew typefaces that were bold statements of typographic reform; he constructed sans serifs and calligraphic faces that broke traditional rules. Late in life, he created Sabon, a classic example of traditional typeface design.

## HOW IT ALL BEGAN

From boyhood, Tschichold was exposed to type, typography, and letterform design. His father, a designer and sign painter, enjoyed his son's company and encouraged him to spend time at his small shop. When he was 12, as a treat, Tschichold's father took him to a big printing and graphic arts trade exposition. It was here that the future typographic radical first saw the work of Europe's best calligraphers and lettering artists. Tschichold was hooked! He knew then that type and letters would always be important to him. First he tried calligraphy. Practicing whenever he had a chance, Tschichold tried to develop his own writing style. As his skills developed, so did his interest in the works of past and present calligraphic masters. The young designer began to study the lettering manuals of Edward Johnston as well as the equally famous, in Germany, Rudolf von Larish.

By the time he was accepted into the Leipzig Academy of Graphic Art and Book Crafts, Tschichold had developed into a capable and prolific calligrapher. He was a serious pupil: He worked hard, practiced his lettering, studied the accepted rules of calligraphy, and learned traditional typographic theory. As a result of his efforts, Tschichold eventually became a graduate student at the academy under the highly regarded German type designer Walter Teimann; and he was entrusted with the responsibility of teaching a class in lettering and calligraphy.

Up until his 22d year, Tschichold's calligraphic and typographic style developed along conservative, if not entirely traditional, lines. He was a "good young designer," just avant-garde enough to be perceived as one of the new generation, but nowhere near radical enough to cause his mentors any concern.

## A NEW SCHOOL OF THOUGHT

Then everything changed. In 1923 Tschichold saw the first major exhibition of the Bauhaus at Weimar—and virtually became an instantaneous convert to the Bauhaus teaching. Like many young converts, Tschichold not only embraced his new religion with zeal, he also felt compelled to renounce vehemently all his earlier ideals. Tschichold completely

AN ATTEMPT TO DEVELOP A SANS SERIF ALPHABET, 1926–29

changed his typographic style, adopting uncompromisingly the new attitudes preached by the Bauhaus. He began to write passionate tracts and articles condemning traditional typographic style. He even temporarily Russianized his name to Ivan in an attempt to further identify himself with the left-wing stance of the Weimar school. The difference between Tschichold and many other young impassioned converts was that people paid attention to him. Tschichold's pleas made a difference. One of his articles, "Elementare Typographie," marks the changing of the face of modern typographic style. In it, and in *Die Neue Typographie,* a small book he published later, Tschichold advocated scrapping all the then popular German types and replacing them with a single sans serif style; and in addition the abandonment of the fashionable style of symmetrical typographic arrangement for asymmetry. His writing and teaching at this period cast Tschichold in the role of a radical. (The contradictions were to come later.)

In the late 1920s, Tschichold emerged as one of the most ardent and uncompromising advocates of modern typography. No dilettante, he was also one of its most skillful exponents. In numerous articles and in hundreds of actual examples, he codified and demonstrated the principles of asymmetrical typographic arrangement. He also designed a "mono-case" (incorporating either capital or lowercase letterforms) sans serif typeface, and published fervent arguments in favor of the use of sans serif type.

## REVOLUTION AGAINST WHAT?

To be fair, Tschichold had a lot of bad typography to react to. The "freie richtung" (free typography) movement of the late 1890s and the Jugenstijl (art nouveau) movement of the early 1900s cluttered German graphic communication with decorative typefaces which at times were almost unreadable, and with a set of typographic rules which hindered, rather than supported, effective communication. Tschichold was reacting to a typographic style that was overly decorative, self-aware, and fussy—at best, mediocre. He believed that one well-designed, straightforward typeface was an infinitely better communicator than all the "fancy types" together; and that facile typographic tricks and affectations should be replaced with the simple dynamism of asymmetrics. Tschichold's work of this period was a reflection of his teaching. His graphic design had an energy and strength that was unprecedented.

Perhaps the most characteristic of Tschichold's work during this period is his poster for the Exhibition of Constructivism, which he designed in 1937. In this piece his exceptionally subtle use of line, graphic elements, and typographic arrangement creates asymmetric dynamism at its best.

For over 15 years, Tschichold created posters, book covers, advertisements, and even letterheads that were quintessential examples of asymmetric design. His work not only created a new typographic genre, it also served as the benchmark of those who followed in his footsteps.

But then something happened. After changing the typographic world and converting countless designers to his way of thinking, Jan Tschichold changed his own mind!

Actually, what Tschichold experienced was more akin to a slow conversion than it was to a spur-of-the-moment change of heart. The results, however, were no less drastic.

## WHY THE CHANGE?

Tschichold's transformation began when he took on commissions to design mass-market books—textbooks, novels, historical fiction, biographies, etc.—instead of posters and his own manuals on typography and graphic design. These were items produced for, and published by, conservative-minded people. Over time, this line of work became Tschichold's main source of income. The more books he designed, the more he realized that one typographic style could not answer all the needs of all typographic applications; and that to insist that the opposite was true

was roughly the equivalent of typographic dictatorship.

Tschichold realized that good typography has to be perfectly legible and, as such, the choices of classical types like Garamond, Jenson, and Baskerville are not only the traditional choice, but also the logical choice for most books. Typographic statements from Tschichold also became much more conservative: "Sans serif is good for certain cases of emphasis, but is now used to the point of abuse. The occasions for using sans serif are as rare as those for using obtrusive decorations." As for asymmetry, Tschichold still considered it to be the most vibrant and stimulating typographic arrangement, but he learned that few of his peers had the talent or discipline to use it correctly. Asymmetric typographic arrangement still held a special attraction for Tschichold, but he became less and less evangelical about converting the world to this design style.

Sadly, Tschichold became the object of typographic ridicule simply for changing his mind. His followers saw in his books, articles, and teaching a way of providing solutions to all typographic problems. Many of them blindly set him up as their "typographic god"—and gods fall very hard from grace.

## FOLLOWERS SPEAK OUT

One disciple, the Swiss architect and designer Max Bill, writing in a German trade magazine, made the impassioned accusation that Tschichold was a renegade from his own teaching, and went on to great lengths to show the contradictions between the gospel for 1928 and Tschichold's later work.

Making his reply some time later in the same periodical, Tschichold sympathizes with the disillusionment felt by his earlier supporters, but asks, in effect, if they would rather he suppress his enlightened beliefs and continue to teach what he no longer felt to be true? He then went on in the article, in a manner typical of the kind teacher, to produce further ex-

EXAMPLE OF THE KIND OF TYPOGRAPHY
TSCHICHOLD WAS REACTING TO DURING
THE EARLY 1900S

amples of his contradictions: ones missed
by Max Bill. Tschichold's circumstance
proves, once again, that there is a heavy
price to pay if you are a revolutionary
(especially a successful one) and continue
to seek the truth beyond simple answers.

## A CHANGE COMPLETED

Tschichold's new classical style was perfected just after World War II. In August
of 1946, the founder of Penguin Books
provided him the opportunity to redesign
the complete Penguin product offering.
This was to be the most extensive and
most difficult challenge of Tschichold's
career.

At the time the publishers of Penguin Books commissioned Tschichold,
they had been using printers scattered
throughout England to produce their
books. Penguin was not staffed for making regular visits to these printers, nor
were they able to respond quickly to the
varied typographic problems they ran
into in the regular course of book produc-

tion. As a result, the printers began to rely
more and more on their own house style
(or in too many cases, whim) to solve
design and typographic problems. The
books suffered. At best they were inconsistent in design and quality; more often,
they were poor examples of typographic
communication.

Immediately upon beginning his
employment at Penguin, Tschichold produced a typographic style manual: a small
booklet that began to outline the basic
guidelines he required. Tschichold recalled that, "It was comparatively easy to
persuade the machine compositors to observe these rules," but that the hand compositors "obviously understood nothing
of what I meant. . . ." He clearly had no
small task on his hands.

One of the guidelines Tschichold
sought was the even spacing of capital letters on title pages. (When setting metal
type by hand, this is a somewhat tedious
and difficult task of hand insertion or
deletion of spacing material—something
which the Penguin compositors preferred
to save themselves the trouble of doing.)
Since Tschichold edited the typography
of every book, he first tried to make simple suggestions to improve character
spacing, but soon was forced to have a
rubber stamp made which printed
"Equalize Letter Spacing According to
Their Optical Value." This tack did not
work either. Tschichold complained that,
"This stamp was practically never noticed." In frustration, he began the tedious, and time consuming, task of writing
by hand individual instructions for every
occasion for which he sought letter spacing improvement. Proof pages were sent
back to the printers littered with phrases
like, "one-half pt. in," or "2 pts. out!"—
and these were only the notes pertaining
to character spacing!

Tschichold edited every page of
every book that Penguin produced. At
first, pages were sent back to printers
with more red than black ink! Gradually,
however, the printers began to understand Tschichold's requirements, and
book quality improved.

vom 16 januar bis 14. februar 1937

kunsthalle basel

**konstruktivisten**

van doesburg
domela
eggeling
gabo
kandinsky
lissitzky
moholy-nagy
mondrian
pevsner
taeuber
vantongerloo
vordemberge
u a

POSTER DESIGNED FOR THE EXHIBITION OF CONSTRUCTIVISM,
1937

CINEMA POSTER, 1928

After he was satisfied that his most basic of composition rules for book production "had been settled and duly propagated," Tschichold went on to reform the design of every Penguin book.

## More Choices

First he made sweeping changes to the typeface repertoire formally supported by Penguin. For the sake of consistency, and probably convenience, all previous Penguin books were set in Times Roman. Tschichold felt that Times was a good newspaper face (indeed, it was originally created as such) but that it was somewhat lacking when it came to book typography. Not "to throw out the baby with the bath," Tschichold did continue to use Times (about 20 percent of the Penguin books continued to be set in the face), but he also widened the composition spectrum to include faces such as Baskerville, Bembo, Garamond, and Caslon. Even the Penguin trademark did not escape Tschichold's attention. After a number of his changes to the book format, the old trademark looked out of place. Tschichold's answer to the problem? Redesign.

Tschichold worked at the Penguin book project for 29 months. At the end, well in excess of 500 books were prepared for printing by his skilled hand—most on a page-by-page basis. Tschichold, himself, stated that his work must have set some kind of typographic world record! During the whole process he never wavered from his standards and never provided anything less than 100 percent commitment to the project. And, as a result, he was completely satisfied with the results. Of the project he wrote, "A publishing firm, that manufactures books in millions to millions, has in any case been able to prove that the cheapest of books can be just as beautifully set and produced as more expensive ones, indeed, even better than most of them!"

## TSCHICHOLD THE TYPE DESIGNER

In addition to being a teacher, typographer, book designer, and rebel, Tschichold was also a typeface designer. While his mono-case sans was not cast as type, and only remains in reproduction of his drawings, two typefaces were designed (and released) in his younger, less conservative years. Transito is a sans serif in the tradition of Futura Black and was created for the Amsterdam type foundry early in the 1930s. It is strictly a display face and saw little use when first issued—and less continued popularity. Shortly after the release of Transito, Tschichold drew Saskia for the Schelter & Giesecke foundry of Leipzig. This too, was a sans serif design, but with much greater calligraphic overtones than his previous design. In fact, the final renderings for the punch cutters were based on letterforms Tschichold drew with a broad-edged pen. The completed design was released in 6- to 60-point type, was more stylish than practical, and enjoyed little popularity outside a small group of Tschichold's followers. Tschichold also produced a number of phototype faces for Uhertype of Berlin, but none survived World War II.

Sabon, a typographic tour de force, is the face that establishes Tschichold's reputation as a type designer.

In the early 1960s, a group of German printers approached Tschichold with a decidedly unique and exceptionally difficult design problem. They sought a type that could be set on either Monotype or Linotype composition equipment, or as handset foundry type, with no perceptible difference in the final product. This meant that all the drawbacks of both Monotype and Linotype composing machines, such things as varying point bodies, kerning restrictions, different unit systems, and duplexing character sets, had to be contended with.

The completed design, released in 1966, not only solved the imposed design problem, it is also an exceptionally beautiful (and useful) design in its own right. So successful was it that, unlike his earlier faces, it continues to be used today, in metal and in photo and digital form.

Sabon has been called "modern Garamond," which is somewhat misleading. Actually, it's not a Garamond, but its own design that was patterned loosely on specimen sheets of the early Frankfurt printer and type founder Konrad Berner. The story is told that Berner married the widow of Jacques Sabon (hence the typeface name) who, it is also said, brought some of Garamond's original matrices to Frankfurt (hence the design similarity to Garamond).

## THE TEACHER'S SIMPLE RULE

When Jan Tschichold died in 1974, the typographic community lost one of its kindest teachers and most gifted practitioners. Tschichold was an artist and craftsperson of the highest order, one who practiced what he preached. He ultimately demanded only one obligation of his followers and students: to organize typographic communication so that it is easy to read and pleasant to view. "Grace in typography," he wrote, "comes of itself when the compositor brings a certain love to his work. Whoever does not love his work cannot hope that it will please others."

# Designers and Their Typefaces

**AICHER**
- Rotis Semi Sans
- Rotis Semi Serif
- Rotis Serif

**ANDRICH**
- Allan
- American Gothic
- Beatrice Script
- Contempo
- Cremona
- Magna Carta
- Vladimir

**AURIOL**
- Auriol

**AUSTIN**
- Bell
- Colonial
- Scotch Roman

**BAKER, A.**
- Amigo
- Marigold
- Oxford
- Pelican
- Visigoth

**BAKER, R.**
- ITC Newtext
- ITC Quorum

**BARTUSKA**
- Caslon No. 641
- News Gothic
- News Gothic Condensed Bold

**BASKERVILLE**
- Baskerville and Italic—Bold

**BAUER, F.**
- Fortuna
- Heyse
- Trennert

**BAUER, K. F.**
- Alpha
- Beta
- Folio (or Caravelle)
- Fortune (or Volta)
- Horizon (or Imprimatur)
- Impressum

**BAUM**
- Alpha
- Beta
- Folio (or Caravelle)
- Fortune (or Volta)
- Horizon (or Imprimatur)
- Impressum

**BELWE**
- Belwe Roman
- Fleischmann
- Shakespeare Mediaeval

**BENGUIAT**
- ITC Barcelona
- ITC Bauhaus (with V. Caruso)
- ITC Benguiat
- ITC Benguiat Gothic
- ITC Bookman
- ITC Caslon 224
- ITC Korinna (with V. Caruso)
- ITC Modern 216
- ITC Modern 216
- ITC Panache
- ITC Souvenir
- ITC Tiffany

**BENTON**
- Antique Shaded
- Century Roman and Italic
- Clearface series
- Lithograph Shaded

**BENTON**
- Adscript
- Agency Gothic
- Alternate Gothic
- American Backslant
- American Caslon and Italic
- American Text
- Announcement Roman and Italic
- Antique Shaded
- Bank Gothic
- Benton (Whitehall)
- Bodoni
- Bold Antique
- Broadway
- Bulfinch Oldstyle
- Bulmer
- Canterbury
- Card Bodoni

- Card Litho
- Card Mercantile
- Card Roman
- Century Bold
- Century Catalogue
- Century Expanded and Italic
- Century Oldstyle
- Century Schoolbook
- Cheltenham
- Chic
- Civilite
- Clearface
- Clearface Gothic
- Clipper
- Cloister Black
- Cloister Oldstyle
- Commercial Script
- Copperplate Gothic Shaded
- Cromwell
- Cushing Antique
- Della Robbia Light
- Dynamic Medium
- Eagle Bold
- Engravers Bodoni
- Engravers Bold
- Engravers Old English
- Engravers Shaded
- Engravers Text
- Franklin Gothic
- Freehand
- Garamond
- Globe Gothic
- Goudy Bold
- Goudy Catalogue
- Goudy Extrabold
- Goudy Handtooled
- Goudy Title
- Gravure
- Greeting Monotone
- Headline Gothic
- Hobo
- Invitation
- Light Hobo
- Light Oldstyle
- Lightline Gothic
- Lithograph Shaded
- Louvaine Light
- Miehle Extra Condensed
- Modernique

Monotone Gothic
Motto
News Gothic
Norwood Roman
Novel Gothic
Othello
Packard
Paramount
Parisian
Parisian Gothic
Pen Print Open
Phenix
Piranesi
Poster Gothic
Raleigh Gothic Condensed
Roycroft
Rugged Roman
Schoolbook Oldstyle
Shadow
Souvenir
Sterling and Cursive
Stymie
Stymie Light
Thermotypes
Tower
Typo Roman
Typo Script
Typo Shaded
Typo Slope
Typo Upright
Venetian
Wedding Text
Whitehall
Whitin Black (or Bold Antique)

**BERNHARD**
Bernhard Booklet
Bernhard Brush Script
Bernhard Cursive (or Madonna)
Bernhard Fashion
Bernhard Gothic
Bernhard Gothic Light
Bernhard Modern Roman
Bernhard Roman
Bernhard Tango
Lilith
Lucian

**BERTHOLD**
Primus

**BIGELOW**
Lucida (with K. Holmes)
Lucida Bright (with K. Holmes)

**BILZ**
Life (with F. Simoncini)

**BINNY**
Binny
Monticello
Oxford

**BLANCHARD**
Garth Graphic (with R. Le Winter)

**BLUMENTHAL**
Emerson

**BOTON**
Agora
Boton
ITC Elan
ITC Eras (with A. Hollenstein)
PE Scherzo

**BRAND**
Albertina

**BRIGHT**
Brighton

**BRIGNALL**
Aachen
Corinthian
Edwardian
Italia
Revue
Romic

**BUDDY**
Roycroft
Tabard

**BULLEN**
Bodoni series
Caslon Oldstyle
Garamond series

**BULMER**
Bulmer

**BURKE**
Aurora
Majestic
Trade Gothic

**BUTTI**
Athenaeum
Cigogna
Fluida
Landi Echo
Microgramma

Normandia
Paganini
Quirinus
Rondine

**CAFLISCH**
Columna

**CALVERT**
Calvert

**CAMPBELL**
ITC Isbell (with R. Isbell)

**CARNASE**
ITC Avant Garde Gothic
(with H. Lubalin)
WTC Carnase Text
WTC Favrile
WTC Goudy
WTC Our Bodoni (with
M. Vignelli)

**CARTER, M.**
Auriga
Bell Centennial
Bitstream Charter
Cascade Script
Cochin
ITC Galliard
Grando Ronde (with H. Hunziker)
Olympian
Shelley Script
Snell
Snell Roundhand
Video

**CARTER, W.**
Klang
Octavian (with D. Kindersley)

**CARUSO**
ITC Bauhaus (with E. Benguiat)
ITC Clearface
ITC Franklin Gothic
ITC Korinna (with E. Benguiat)

**CASLON**
Caslon and Italic
Caslon Text

**CASSANDRE**
Acier Noir
Bifur
Peignot
Touraine

**CHAPPELL**
Lydian
Trajanus

**CLELAND**
Caslon Swash
Della Robbia
Garamond
Westminister Old Style
(or Della Robbia)

**COCHIN**
Nicolas Cochin

**COOPER**
Boul Mich
Cooper Black
Cooper Old Style
Dietz Text
Packard
Pompeian Cursive

**CRAW**
Ad Lib
Craw Clarendon
Craw Modern

**CUSHING**
Cushing
Norwood Roman

**DAIR**
Cartier

**DEMETER**
Demeter
Fournier
Hollandisch
Pearl Fournier

**DEROSS**
Card Italic
De Ross
Egmont
Ella
Erasmus
Hollandse Mediaeval
Libra
Medieval
Meidoorn
Simplex
Zilver Type

**DETTERER**
Eusebius

**DEVINNE, T.L.**
Century
Century Roman
DeVinne series
Renner

**DIDOT**
French Round Face

**DIETHELM**
Diethelm Roman
Sculptura

**DISPIGNA**
ITC Serif Gothic (with H. Lubalin)

**DOM**
Dom

**DOMBREZIAN**
Dom Casual & Diagonal—Bold

**DOOIJES**
Contura
Lectura
Mercator
Rondo

**DUENSING**
Chancery Italic
Quadrata II
Rustica
Sixteenth Century Roman

**DWIGGINS**
Calendonia
Eldorado
Electra
Falcon
Metro

**ENGELMANN**
ITC Golden Type (with H.
Joergensen and A. Newton)

**ERBAR**
Candida
Erbar
Feder Grotesk
Koloss

**EXCOFFON**
Antique Olive
Banco
Calypso
Chambord
Choc

Diane
Mistral

**FORSBERG**
Berling
Carolus
Lunda
Parad

**FOURNIER**
Fournier
Fournier le Jeune

**FRIZ**
Friz Quadrata

**FRUTIGER**
Apollo
Avenir
Breughel
Frutiger
Glypha
Icone
Iridium
Linotype Centennial
Meridian
OCR-B
Ondine
Opera
Phoebus
President
Serifa
Tiemann (adapted from the work
of Walter Tiemann)
Univers
Versailles

**GARAMOND**
Garamond
Garamont

**GILL**
Floriated Capitals
Gill Sans
Golden Cockerel Type
Joanna
Perpetua
Pilgrim
Solus

**GOODHUE**
Chelthenham
Merrymount

**GOUDY**
Aries
Bertham

Booklet Old Style
Californian and Italic
Camelot
Caxton Initials
Collier Old Style
Companion Old Style and Italic
Copperplate Gothic
Copperplate Gothic Heavy
Cushing Antique
Cushing Italic
Deepdene
DeVinne Roman
Forum
Forum Capitals
Foster Abstract
Frenchwood Ronde (or
Italian Old Style)
Friar
Garamond
Garamont
Globe Gothic Bold
Goudy Antique
Goudy Cursive
Goudy Extra Bold
Goudy Heavyface
Goudy Lanston
Goudy Light Old Style
Goudy Modern
Goudy Old Style
Goudy Open & Italic
Goudy Ornate
ITC Goudy Sans
Goudy Sanserif
Goudy Stout
Goudy Text
Goudy Thirty
Goudytype
Goudy Village
Hadriano
Hearst
Italian Old Style
Kaatskill
Kennerley
Kennerly Old Style
Klaxon
Lombardic Caps
Marlborough
Mediaeval
Nabisco
National Old Style
Norman Capitals
Pabst Old Style and Italic

Pabst Roman
Powell
Record Title
Remington Typewriter
Saks Goudy
Sans Serif
Scripps College Old Style
Sherman
Tory Text
Trajan Title
Truesdell
University of California Old Style
Venezia
Venizia Italic
Village
Village Text

**GRANJON**
Granjon and Italic
Plantin and Italic

**GRIFFITH**
Corona
Bell Gothic
Excelsior
Granjon Bold
Ionic Condensed
Ionic No. 5
Janson
Monticello
Opticon & Italic
Paragon
Poster Bodoni
Ryerson Condensed
Textype

**GRIFFO**
Bembo

**GSCHWIND**
Media (with A. Gurtler and
C. Mengelt)
Signa (with A. Gurtler and
C. Mengelt)
Haas Unica (with A. Gurtler and
C. Mengelt)

**GURTLER**
Basilia
Egyptian 505
Media (with E. Gschwind and
C. Mengelt)
Signa (with E. Gschwind and
C. Mengelt)
Haas Unica

**HAMMER**
Andromaque
Hammer Uncial

**HARLING**
Playbill

**HARTZ**
Emergo
Juliana
Mole Foliate

**HARVEY**
Ellington

**HAUS**
Guardi

**HAVINDEN**
Ashley Crawford
Ashley Script

**HAYDEN–DUENSING**
Chancery Cursive
Rustica
XVIth Century Roman

**HESS**
Alternate Gothic Modernized
Artscript
Bookman Old Style Condensed
Bruce Old Style and Italic
Caslon Old Style No. 437
Cochin
Copper Tooled
English Caslon No. 37
Flash
Goudy Bible
Goudy Bold Swash
Hadriano Stone-Cut
Hess Bold
Hess Monoblack
Hess Neobold
Hess New Bookbold
Hess Old Style
Hess Title
Italian Old Style Wide
Janson
Jefferson Gothic
Kennerley Open Caps
Laurentian
New Bookman
Onyx Italic
Pendrawn
Postblack Italic
Post-Stout Italic

**HESS** *(Cont.)*
Poster
Sans Serif
Slimline
Spire
Squareface
Stationers Gothic
Stylescript
Stymie
Tourist Gothic
20th Century
Ward

**HOEFER**
Elegance
Monsoon
Permanent
Saltino
Salto
Zebra

**HOLLANDSWORTH**
Hiroshige
ITC Tiepolo

**HOLLENSTEIN**
ITC Eras (with A. Boton)

**HOLMES**
Isadora
Lucida (with C. Bigelow)
Lucida Bright (with C. Bigelow)
Shannon (with J. Prescott)
Sierra

**HUGHES**
Century Nova

**HUNZIGER, H.**
Grando Ronde (with M. Carter)

**HUXLEY**
Huxley Vertical

**ISBELL**
Americana
ITC Isbell (with J. Campbell)

**JAEGER**
Aja
Bellevue
Catull
Chasseur
Cornet
Cosmos
Daily News
Delta

Epikur
Jaeger–Antiqua
Jersey
Jumbo
Osiris
Seneca

**JAMRA**
ITC Jamille

**JANNON**
Garamond and Italic

**JANSON**
Janson

**JENSON**
Centaur
Cloister series
Eusebius series
Hess Old Style
Jenson Oldstyle
Montaigne

**JOERGENSEN**
ITC Golden Type (with S.
Engelmann and A. Newton)

**JONES**
Crillee

**JOHNSTON**
Imprint
Johnston's Railway Type
(or Underground)

**JONES**
Georgina
Granjon

**JOST**
Aeterna (or Jost Mediaeval)
Beton

**KADAN, J.**
ITC American Typewriter
(with T. Star)

**KAUFMANN**
Balloon (or Lasso)
Kaufmann
Kaufmann Script

**KINDERSLEY**
Itek Bookface
Octavian (with W. Carter)

**KLEUKENS**
Helga (or Olga)
Kleukens Antique

Omega
Ratio Roman
Scriptura

**KLUMPP**
Catalina
Murray Hill

**KOCH**
Cable (or Kabel)
Holla
Jessen
Koch Kurrent
Locarno (or Koch Antiqua)
Marathon
Maximilian Antiqua
Neuland
Offenbach
Steel
Wallau

**LANGE**
AG Buch Stencil
AG Old Face
Arena
Baskerville Book
Berthold Script
Bodoni Old Face
Boulevard
Calson Buch
Champion
Concorde
Concorde Nova
Derby
El Greco
Franklin Antiqua
Garamond
Imago
Solemnis
Walbaum Buch
Walbaum Standard

**LE WINTER**
Garth Graphic (with C. Blanchard)

**LUBALIN**
ITC Avant Garde Gothic (with
T. Carnase)
ITC Lubalin Graph
ITC Serif Gothic (with
A. DiSpigna)

**MCMURTRIE**
McMurtrie Title
Ultra Modern

**MANUTIUS**
Bembo
Cloister Italic

**MARDERSTEIG**
Dante
Fontana
Griffo
Zeno

**MATT**
Matt Antique

**MEDINGER**
Helvetica
Horizontal
Pro Arte

**MEEKS**
Bramley
Plaza

**MEIER**
Syntax

**MENDOZA Y ALMEIDA**
ITC Mendoza Roman
Pascal
Photina

**MENGELT**
Media (with E. Gschwind and
A. Gurtler)
Signa
Haas Unica

**MENHART**
Ceska Unciala
Figural
Manuscript
Menhart
Menhart Roman
Monument
Parliament
Triga
Victory

**MEYER**
Syntax

**MEYNELL**
Imprint

**MIDDLETON**
Admiral Script
Andromaque
Cameo
Condensed Gothic Outline

Coronet
Delphian Open Titling or Title
Eden
Eusebius
Flair
Florentine Cursive
Formal Script
Garamond
Karnak
Karnak Light
Lafayette
Ludlow Black
Mandate
Mayfair Cursive
Radiant
Radiant Medium
Record Gothic
Samson
Square Gothic
Stellar
Stencil
Tempo
Umbra
Wave

**MOLLENSTADT**
Formata

**MOORE**
Post Oldstyle No. 1 and
Italic—No. 2

**MORISON WITH LARDENT**
Times New Roman

**MORRIS**
Chaucer
Collier Old Style
Golden Type
Jenson Oldstyle Italic
Morris Romanized Black
Troy

**NEWTON**
ITC Golden Type (with S.
Engelmann and H. Joergensen)

**NICHOLAS**
Nimrod

**NORTON**
Else

**NOVARESE**
Arbiter
Athenaeum
Cigno

Colossal
Egizio
Elite
Estro
Eurostile
Expert
ITC Fenice
Fontanesi
Forma
Garaldus
Juliet
Lapidar
Magister
Metropol
Microgramma
ITC Mixage
ITC Novarese
Oscar
Recta
Slogan
Stop
ITC Symbol

**PACELLA**
ITC Cushing
ITC Pacella

**PEIGNOT**
Garamont

**PEIGNOT**
Cristal

**PERRIN**
Lyons Titling

**PETERS**
Angelus
Castellar
Fleet Titling
Traveller

**PHINNEY**
Abbott Oldstyle
Bradley
Camelot
Cloister Black
Cheltenham Oldstyle
Flemish
Globe Gothic
Jensen (or Italian Old Style)
Jensen Oldstyle
Oxford & Italic
Satanick
Taylor Gothic

**PIERPONT**
Plantin

**PISCHNER**
Stempel Sans (or Neuzeit
Grotesque)

**PLANTIN**
Plantin

**POPPL**
Poppl–Antiqua
Poppl–College
Poppl–Exquisit
Poppl–Laudatio
Poppl–Nero
Poppl–Pontifex
Poppl–Residenz

**POST**
Dynamic
Post Marcato
Post Mediaeval
Post Roman

**POWELL**
Onyx (or Arsis)
Stymie

**PRESCOTT**
Shannon (with K. Holmes)

**QUAY**
Helicon
Quay
ITC Quay Sans

**REINER**
Bazaar
Contact
Crovinus
Florida
London Script
Matura
Mercurius
Meridian
Mustang
Pepita
Reiner Black
Reiner Script
Stradivarius

**RENNER**
Futura
Topic (or Steile Futura)

**ROGERS**
Bell and Italic
Centaur
Goudy Bible
Italian Old Style
Janson
Goudy Bible
Montaigne

**RONALDSON**
Oxford

**RUZICKA**
Fairfield and Italic—Medium and
Italic
Primer and Italic

**SACK**
Proteus
Stratford (with A. Williams)

**SALLWEY**
Present

**SALTER**
Flex

**SCHNEIDLER**
Deutsch Romisch
Graphik (or Herald)
Kontrast
Legend
Schneidler Old Style
(or Bauer Text)

**SCHWEIZER**
Dominante

**SCHWEDTNER**
Metropolis
Mundus

**SHAAR**
Flash
Futura Demibold Script
Futura Extra Bold
Imperial
Royal
Satellite
Valiant
Windsor

**SIEGEL**
Adobe Tekton

**SIMOCINI**
Aster
Delia

**SLIMBACH**
Adobe Garamond
ITC Giovanni
Adobe Minion
ITC Simbach
Adobe Utopia

**SMITH**
Brush
Park Avenue

**SNIFFIN**
Hollywood
Keynote
Liberty
Nubian
Piranesi
Raleigh Cursive
Rivoli
Rosetti

**SPIEKERMANN**
Berliner Grotesk
Lo-Type
ITC Officina

**STAN**
ITC American Typewriter
(with J. Kadan)
ITC Berkeley Old Style
ITC Century
ITC Cheltenham
ITC Garamond
Pasquale

**STONE**
ITC Stone Formal
ITC Stone Sans
ITC Stone Serif
ITC Stone Print

**THANNHAEUSER**
Adastra
Erler Titling
Gravira
Kurier
Liberta
Lotto
Meister
Parcival
Thannhaeuser

**THOMPSON**
Baltimore Script
Collier Heading

Futura
Mademoiselle
Thompson Quillscript

**TIEMANN**
Daphnis
Offizin
Orpheus
Tiemann
Tiemann Mediaeval

**TRAVY**
Jubilee
Lintotype Modern
Maximus
Modern
Times Europa

**TRAFTON**
Cartoon (or Tresko)
Trafton Script

**TREACY**
Bryn Mawr

**TRENHOLM**
Cornell & Italic
Egmont Decorative Initials
Georgian Cursive
Nova Script
Trenholm Initials
Trenholm Old Style

**TRUMP**
Amati
City
Codex
Delphin
Forum
Jaguar
Mauritius
Palomba
Schadow
Signum
Time
Trump Mediaeval

**TSCHICHOLD**
Sabon
Saskia
Transito

**TWOMBLY**
Adobe Charlemagne
Adobe Lithos

Mirarae
Adobe Trajan

**TYFA**
Kolektiv
Tyfa

**UNGER**
Bitstream Amerigo
Cyrano
Demos
Flora
Hollander
Praxis
Swift

**USHERWOOD**
Administer
Caxton
Flange
ITC Leawood
Lynton
Marbrook
ITC Usherwood

**VAN KRIMPEN**
Cancellaresca Bastarda
Haarlemmer
Lutetia
Open Roman Capitals
Romanee
Romulus
Spectrum
Van Dujck

**VELJOVIC**
ITC Esprit
ITC Gamma
ITC Veljovic

**VIGNELLI**
WTC Our Bodoni (with
T. Carnase)

**VOLLENWEIDER**
Rotunda

**WARDE**
Arrighi
Arrighi Italic

**WEIDEMANN**
ITC Weidemann

**WEISS**
Weiss Roman
Weiss Rundgotisch

**WEISS**
Memphis

**WIEBKING**
Artcraft

**WILKE**
Ariston
Burgund
Caprice
Discus
Gladiola
Konzept
Palette

**WILLIAMS**
Claridge
Congress
Leamington
Raleigh
Seagull
Stratford (with F. Sack)
Trieste
Worcester Round

**WINKOW**
Alcazar
Electra
Iberica
Nacional
Reporter

**WOLPE**
Albertus
Hyperion
Pegasus

**ZAPF-VON HESSE**
Ariadne
Bitstream Carmina
Diotima
Nofret
Smaragd

**ZAPF**
Aldus
Aurelia
Comenius
Edison
Hunt Toma
Kompakt
Marconi
Medici Script
Melior

**ZAPF** *(Cont.)*
Mergenthaler
Noris Script
Optima
Orion

Palatino
Sapphire
Vario
Venture
Venture Script

Virtuosa
ITC Zapf Book
ITC Zapf Chancery
ITC Zapf International
Zapf Renaissance